MW00877568

# IS THE J U I C E WORTH THE SQUEEZE?

The Valuable Habit of Learning from
Your Business Experiences

To Tom
Happy Reading
& Saving, Too

# GEORGE E. CASEY, JR.

ISBN 1452891389
ISBN-13: 9781452891385

# DEDICATION

*To Bob Toll, who taught me that a wise man knows what he doesn't know; to my wife, Linda Bail, who allowed me the space and provided the encouragement to create this book; and to my sons, Peter and Matthew, to hopefully encourage them to keep learning, coaching, and teaching in their careers, too.*

*The most difficult subjects can be explained to the most slow-witted man if he has not formed any idea of them already; but the simplest thing cannot be made clear to the most intelligent man if he is firmly persuaded that he knows already, without a shadow of doubt, what is laid before him.*

*— Leo Tolstoy, 1897*

# TABLE OF CONTENTS

# FOREWORD

A habit is defined as an action or pattern of behavior that is repeated so often that it becomes typical of somebody, although he or she may be unaware of it. There are good habits and bad habits. We usually try to develop the good ones and get rid of the bad ones.

In a career as a leader and a manager, I have found that one of the best habits to develop is how to learn in an everyday working environment. Even more important, though, is the ability to teach others the skill of everyday learning. Inside of organizations, this habit can create great positive force if the learning can be made part of a culture and the lessons learned applied so that individuals and the organization make more good judgments and decisions than bad ones.

My technique for the transmission of wisdom is a catchy phrase or simple story that people can remember. What I have found is that such simple mechanisms can be remembered for decades, and the lessons attached to them are then remembered, too.

The ability to learn from experience can become a habit. This book is written to encourage younger managers and students of business to help to develop that habit. I have chosen about thirty of the business lessons I have learned through my career as examples.

In their own right, they are helpful reminders for the reader.

I have also included at the end of each chapter an exercise question that serves as a discussion topic for both individuals and groups to probe a topic related to each chapter's lesson point. In so doing, my goal is for people to begin to develop their own summary phrases or stories that embody some wisdom learned that could be passed on to others.

It is the beginning of trying to form the habit for the reader.

My working career has been primarily in the home-building and community development industries, with occasional sojourns into consulting assignments in other types of business and a four-year tour in the Navy's Civil Engineer Corps.

After my four years on active duty in the Navy, I headed to business school at the Wharton School of the University of Pennsylvania in Philadelphia. Business school in those days was competitive, but there was more of a pure academic bent to it than there is today.

There was this built-in expectation that you first learned all that you could in your two years at Wharton, and that for the rest of your career you were expected to not only apply that learning, but also continue to learn from your experiences and then to pass that accumulated learning on to those who worked with and for you.

Although not formally stated as such, you felt that there was a lifetime obligation that was part of the privilege of attending one of the best business education programs in the world.

Business was presented to us as both an art and a science dedicated to getting things done through the common efforts of many. As a master of that art and science, part of your duty was to advance and disseminate that knowledge to whatever spheres of influence you could.

Even in my naval officer career before business school, I found that managing by walking around was natural for me. Being Irish and from the Boston area, I think some of the skills of being a good ward politician rubbed off. I enjoyed being with and talking to the people who worked with me and for me.

I got in the habit of asking a simple question: "What did you learn today?" It was a great, open-ended question that was nonthreatening and led to easy conversation. I could see what that person was working on and see if it was an effort in the direction I was trying to take my team, division, or company.

Since people knew that I asked the question, they began to think more about what they actually were learning from what they were doing or seeing done around them. That learning helped them to grow and helped me to absorb nuances of the business as seen through multiple engaged eyes and brains.

As I advanced in management responsibility, I began to take the lessons I was learning about the business we were doing and developed a habit of teaching those lessons to younger managers and then broader groups in my company and at industry conferences. Along the way, I stumbled on usually simple phrases and stories that I could use to headline a concept. Those phrases and stories, sometimes humorous, would then serve as the keywords for the broader group to remember the concept, many times decades later.

It provided a simple code for a discussion or reminder.

After several years of doing this work, people who had worked for me would easily recall the lessons, stories, and code words, and would often comment that the concept had helped them in their career, and they, in turn, were passing the concept on. It was pretty heady stuff.

Usually, at some point in the conversation, the phrase "you should write a book about this stuff" would come forth, and I would nod, smile, and keep on doing whatever job I was undertaking at that point.

In the spring of 2009, while working in Phoenix for DMB Associates, the large community developer, I noticed that my finance manager, Aaron Macneil, had been copying down my expressions ("Georgeisms" he called them) in the back of a journal that he carried with him. One day, he asked if I would write down all the "Georgeisms" that I recalled. Combining my list with his, we came up with a master list. At the same time, Charley Freericks, DMB's vice president for talent, encouraged me to take the list and circulate it among some of the other managers. From that circulation came more encouragement to write them down, expand upon them, and to perhaps put them in book form.

That encouragement has led to this endeavor to take some of the simple lessons and wisdom that I wish someone had taught me earlier in my career and to document them in a manner that is simple and straightforward.

By setting forth these "lessons learned the hard way," I hope that others might apply them to their career and their management of people and organizations, hopefully for the better.

Even more, I hope that this encourages readers to think about the lessons they learn from their experiences and to create their own phrases and stories that they, in turn, can use to pass on wisdom learned to others.

It is a great habit to both have and pass on. From the sometimes bitter fruits of experience, the juices of wisdom can be squeezed.

# I

## WISDOM

*Think about the number of times that you have been in a meeting and you have no idea what the speaker is talking about. Yet the others in the meeting are nodding their heads in assent, seeming to indicate that they do understand. The social pressure is intense to also nod, even if you are getting more confused by the second. It is a brave person who raises his or her hand and says, "I don't understand. Can you explain that again?" The more experienced one becomes as a manager, the more one appreciates those who have the fortitude to slow or stop things so that the topic is fully understood and the fine points are examined.*

It was 1992 and I was the chief financial officer of Realen Homes, a private residential builder/developer in Pennsylvania. We were weathering the economic downturn of the early 1990s, precipitated by the collapse of the savings and loan banks across the country. The new regulations that were evolving required real estate developers to have more equity in their businesses than they had before.

Furthermore, some of the distressed real estate projects that were being sold by banks and the government were being priced at steep discounts, thereby offering the potential for profits in the future once the market did return. But, in order to purchase those projects, Realen would need more money than it currently had.

The owners of Realen had tasked me with trying to bring more equity into the company, perhaps by taking the company public through an initial public offering of stock. As a part of the process, I worked on finding a good securities law firm in Philadelphia to work with us before we lined up an investment banker.

In one of the first interviews with one of the lead securities attorneys, he was reviewing some of the deals that they had been involved with that were similar to what our deal would probably look like. I had not come from the securities and finance side of the world; I had primarily been an operations person up to that point.

Even though I had an MBA in finance and knew the basic language of finance, I was still a relative babe in the woods. In one of the early parts of the discussion, the attorney kept mentioning that the company had decided to issue "X" number of shares of stock with a 15 percent "Green Shoe." My head was spinning trying to figure out why someone was wearing green shoes or how shoes had anything to do with finance.

Finally, I interrupted the attorney and said: "Listen, I am pretty dumb, and so I am going to ask a lot of questions that may slow you down a bit, but it is the only way I can learn. What is a 'Green Shoe'?"

He then told me that it was an extra allocation of stock that was authorized to be sold at the discretion of the banker if the demand for the stock was good or if they needed it to stabilize pricing in the post-IPO market. If we were issuing 2,000,000 shares with a 15% "Green Shoe" it meant that the banker could actually sell up to 2,300,000 shares, if there was demand or need for the shares.

I then asked him why it was called a "Green Shoe." He told me that it was called that because the first time the technique had been used was for a stock offering for the Green Shoe Manufacturing Company (the ancestor to the Stride Rite Corporation) and, thereafter, it was called a "Green Shoe."

With that under my belt, we could continue.

I was applying the basic lesson of "It is a wise man who knows what he does not know." Sometimes stated as "The only thing I know is that which I do not know" or "To be wise, the only thing you really need to know is when to say 'I don't know,' " this simple observation has been attributed to Socrates, Lao Tzu, and various Indian mystics.

I learned it from Bob Toll, the chairman and chief executive officer of Toll Brothers. Bob has a master's of law from the University of Pennsylvania and is a great hands-on teacher.

In my first week as a project manager at Toll Brothers in 1979, Bob had me in his office and we were reviewing a contract for the sale of a house. Bob would take a paragraph at random from the contract and ask me to interpret what the paragraph said. He would then commence to ask question upon question, peeling the onion if you would, about the topic and very quickly arriving at the point that I did not know the answer to the asked question.

His objective was to take away the fear of saying "I don't know."

He drove home the point that the humility to accept that you did not know all the answers was the first step in making sure that you understood (and understood fully) a topic. "Be dumb," he counseled. By not being afraid to admit that you don't know and then having the discipline of asking questions until you do know, the chances of overlooking some important issue in a business deal are greatly diminished.

The key to the whole lesson was having the humility to admit without shame that you did not know the answer. If you did not have that humility and, instead, rushed past an issue, nodding "Got it," you opened yourself to missing the fine points that could either come back to haunt you later or cause you to miss an opportunity. It also limited your learning on a long-term basis.

So, of the lessons not regularly taught in business school, the humility of knowing when you don't know and then having the gumption to ask deep, probing questions until you do know has to stand as one of the most important of all.

And a special thanks to Bob Toll for teaching that one.

**"It is a wise man who knows what
he does not know."**

Exercise: Have you had a recent experience where you did not know what someone was talking about? How did you handle it? Why?

_____

_____

_____

_____

_____

_____

_____

_____

_____

_____

_____

_____

_____

_____

_____

_____

_____

_____

_____

_____

# 2

## MORE AND FASTER

*Have you ever been in a situation where you have to make a business judgment, but you don't have your computer or your calculator? There are some pretty simple rules of thumb to help you decide, just the way that Carnegie, Mellon, and Rockefeller did before the days of computers and calculators.*

Net Present Value and its cousin, Internal Rate of Return, are mathematical calculations that attempt to determine the relative worth of investments.

The concept is pretty simple: a dollar today is worth a dollar. However, a dollar received a year from now is worth less because you had to wait to get it and, during that waiting period, if you had already had the dollar, you could have invested it.

For example, if you could invest money at 6 percent, a dollar today is worth $1.06 a year from now. So for an investment received a year from now, it would have to be worth more than $1.06 in order to be more valuable than receiving a dollar today.

These concepts of time, interest rate, and amount received get much more complicated when multiple different amounts are received at different points in time. Before the days of computers, the calculations were pretty laborious in order to determine which stream of competing cash flows was more valuable. They were done by hand, using tables.

With the advent of computers and financial calculators, the complex calculations are relatively easy to perform and to model. Any MBA worth his or her salt knows how to model an investment or a project on Excel and how to do multiple scenarios to determine which provides the best "risk adjusted" investment return. For quicker and simpler calculations, financial calculators enable managers to do in seconds that which took hours by longhand.

However, with the advent of all of these easy mechanical and electronic means of performing net present value and internal rate of return calculations, the basics of why you do the calculations and the limitations of the method have gotten lost in the shuffle for many.

Presented with some facts or assumptions, the immediate reflex is to "model it" when, in fact, one can come to a basic conclusion without the modeling. One forgets that some of the best business minds in the world operated pretty well before the days of calculators, spreadsheets, and calculus-based theories. Somehow they were able to make business decisions involving money and time that worked out pretty well (see Rockefeller and Carnegie for proof).

After personally using net present value calculations for a career, helped on, thankfully, by the creation of the HP12c Financial Calculator, one understands that net present value can really be taught and understood in about thirty seconds.

My friend and fellow Wharton graduate Joe Duckworth summed it up with great simplicity one day:

"More is better than less. Sooner is better than later. And the higher the cost of capital, the more it is true."

That was it.

When you think about it, this applies primarily to cash coming in. The more you can get sooner, the better off you will be. A dollar received a year from now is worth less than a dollar received today; much less if the cost of capital is high.

Of course, the corollary is also true for cash going out. That is, "Less is better than more, and later is better than sooner." If you can defer the payment of cash until later, it is usually better for you.

The more your money costs (or the higher the rate of return for alternative investments), the more important timing is. If it is cash coming in the door, with high rates, dollars four or five years out (or longer) aren't worth very much, and their impact on a decision is small. You have to know in relative detail only what is happening in the first couple of years to understand the basics of the investment.

On the other hand, if the analysis involves cash going out the door and high costs of capital, the impact of those outflows is pretty small in the present value analysis if the cost of capital is high.

In one of my "what are you learning today" questions to a financial analyst, I was taught a great rule of thumb: divide 100 by the cost of capital in order to get an idea of how many years are really important to an evaluation.

For example, if your cost of capital is high (say 25 percent), the first four years of an investment

(100 divided by 25 equals 4) is all that you really need to look at. Anything happening after the fourth year will have very little impact on the return. On the other hand, if the cost of capital is 10 percent, anything happening in the first ten years has to be evaluated, with events in the first couple of years having a stronger impact than the later years. It is a rough measure, but it works.

So, if your computer goes down or your calculator battery goes dead and you have to make a judgment based on common sense, Joe's simple lesson usually applies.

**"*More is better than less. Sooner is better than later. And the higher the cost of capital, the more it is true.*"**

Exercise: Are there some simple observations that you can make about making financial decisions that are good rules of thumb to pass on to others? What are they?

_____

_____

_____

_____

_____

_____

_____

_____

_____

_____

_____

_____

_____

_____

_____

_____

_____

_____

_____

# 3

# THE MARKET

*Have you ever been in a quandary as to how to price your product or service? There is a pretty simple rule and some basic ideas that will help you decide.*

MBAs spend a lot of time figuring out what something should sell for. You learn cost accounting, markup theory, how to derive demand curves, marginal cost and benefit, and a whole lot of other techniques that try to give guidance regarding what you should sell your product for.

Business is the simple act of figuring out what people want and delivering it to them at a price that is ideally greater than the cost of producing the product. If you do that, you have a business. If you don't, you have a hobby, a charity, or an enterprise on its way to extinction. It is that simple.

The hard part is truly figuring out what people will pay for your product. Different people will pay different amounts for the same product based on the product's value to them. The classic example is Federal Express (FedEx) and the U.S. Postal Service (USPS). You can pay 44 cents to have a letter delivered to someone in somewhere between two and seven days, depending on the vicissitudes of the USPS. On the other hand, FedEx will guarantee a delivery the next day by 10 a.m. But it costs around $10. For someone who absolutely has to have a document there tomorrow, FedEx's $10 is a bargain. However, if the document is marginally valuable and time is not an issue, the USPS's 44 cents is a heck of a bargain.

Different values apply to different users based upon their particular and individual circumstances at a given point in time.

Figuring out what the market will bear for your product is really an act of experimentation: trying, testing, learning, modifying, and then doing it again. The more frequently and intelligently you can do it, the better off you will most likely be.

I can remember early in my homebuilding career at Toll Brothers, we used to set house prices three times a year. We would study our competition and what they were doing, study our costs and margins, and try to determine pricing that made us competitive with other builders and gave us satisfactory margins. We would then implement the pricing and, four months later, take a look at what had happened and repeat the exercise.

Later, we began to look at pricing a little bit differently. We had targeted sales rates and would adjust pricing more frequently, depending on selling rates, in order to meet the sales goals. It was a more frequent testing of what the market would bear, and we could adjust much more quickly based upon what the market was bearing at that point in time.

In doing this quicker adjustment, we began to learn why we (or our competition) sold better and began to adjust not only pricing, but product also (both the physical product and the service packages included with the product). We were trying to find what the market would bear.

My finance director at DMB, Aaron Macneil, told a story of auditing a company that was in the billboard sign business. It was earlier in his career as an auditor at one of the large public accounting firms. The billboard company was highly successful and profitable. As part of the audit, auditors asked for the price list that the company used for its board rentals. The CEO responded that he did not have one. Instead, the company tried to determine the relative importance of the board and its location to the potential customer and the importance of obtaining the rental contract at that moment in time for their company, given the current environment. The head of the company then determined the price he thought he should get, given those circumstances, and negotiated hard for that price. It worked well for him, but confounded the auditors, who were looking for a fixed price list and could not find one.

Again, Joe Duckworth, in his simplification of the basic truth for this situation, said it best: "Never charge less than the market will bear."

It seems simple enough, but it is often overlooked. In spite of all of the analysis that one can do, all of the research that one can compile and purchase, and all of the experts one can consult, the best test of pricing is to try it and then see what you learn and, from that learning, adjust pricing again.

When Apple first brought out iTunes, it took 99 cents as a price point for a song as a starting point, figuring that a buck for a song was a pretty nominal amount. After testing the model for a while, Apple began to see that it could charge more ($1.29 or $1.99) for highly popular songs and less ($0.66) for less popular songs.

The feedback from sales in its electronic store allowed it to see this pattern and to begin testing different pricing levels and strategies. Apple was, in a very organized and data-rich way, determining what the market would bear at a given point in time and for different kinds of products. I would not be surprised to see the company eventually evolve to even more dynamic pricing models in the future.

Some of the more sophisticated toll roads have already arrived at that point. With transponders that automatically pay tolls, some of the toll-way managers have figured out that the "instant toll" for the express lane is worth more at various points of the rush hour. By being able to see what demand is for the express lane is on a real-time basis, toll rates are adjusted upward when the lane starts to become crowded at rush hour, and then the rate starts to come down again as the demand drops at the end of rush hour.

The more that technology is able to provide quick feedback on demand and tools are available to change pricing quickly, the more enterprises can learn about the value of their product to various market segments and at various times. This information and pricing action can then lead to higher profitability over time.

So, the simple lesson is:

## "Never charge less than what the market will bear."

Exercise: Are there general rules of thumb that you use or have used to price your product or to adjust pricing on your product? What are they? Can you condense them to a quick or memorable phrase or story?

_____

_____

_____

_____

_____

_____

_____

_____

_____

_____

_____

_____

_____

_____

_____

_____

_____

_____

_____

_____

# 4

## JUMBO SHRIMP

*Are you involved with doing promotions as part of a marketing campaign for your company? There are some simple truths that will help you to get positive value out of the time, money, and effort that you put into your promotions.*

Most businesses have an element of promotion to them. (We will discuss that *P* later in the book along with a lot of other *P*s.) Letting people know about you, your product, your organization, and the individuals who make up your organization is an important building block for any successful business.

How you promote has a lot to say about you and how your organization values your customers. Great promotions create buzz that helps to tip the balance in favor of your product or company. Failed promotions can actually damage a company's brand by demonstrating either a lack of planning or a lack of understanding of your product or customer.

The bottom line is that promotion can be either a beneficial or a treacherous undertaking. You can win big and get value far in excess of cost. You can also lose big and spend a lot of money and actually damage your reputation.

In the real estate development and homebuilding businesses I have been involved with, the terrain is not much different than for any other business undertaking. There are wholesale elements to the business and definitely retail elements. As a developer, you "wholesale" finished lots to homebuilders or commercial builders, who build buildings or homes for retail sale to end users.

As a homebuilder, even though you retail sell homes to individuals, rarely do those individuals buy multiple homes from you over the course of their life. They may refer others and occasionally may buy another home from you, but the nature of the business is that those events are in the minority. The true influencers of individual purchases in most markets in the country are the army of residential Realtors®, who act as the experienced intermediaries between a builder/seller and a buyer. In some markets, nearly 90 percent of new home sales involve a Realtor®. They are a hugely influential piece of the sales chain and a critical ally to have.

Consequently, successful builders and developers tend to promote heavily to Realtors, so that the Realtors (on behalf of the future customers they will service) understand the builder's products, pricing, value proposition, and so forth. Whether it is via outings to ball games, contests, or presentations to agents regarding a new home design or a new neighborhood, the goal is to have a developed and deep relationship with Realtors in the hope of at least having a chance to sell a house when they have customers who are potential buyers for your product.

In building the new town of Weston in South Florida, Arvida acted both as the homebuilder and developer for the community. At its peak in the late 1990s and early 2000s, Weston was selling and building between one thousand and seventeen hundred homes per year, and nearly 70 percent of our business involved Realtors. With over a dozen product lines and opening new phases and products regularly, positive relationships with the Realtor community were critical.

The director of marketing for Arvida was a wise man, Dick Larsen. Dick had worked on many of the Arvida communities that had literally created the town of Boca Raton, Florida. He was experienced, savvy, funny, and insightful. He was a Realtor and knew the species well, also.

Dick and his event planner, Mary Peich, were like a machine. Model grand openings, phase grand openings, and broker appreciation events were all part of their repertoire. Model grand openings involved the introduction of a new home design or a series of designs. Phase openings were for when we brought a new neighborhood (typically fifty to one hundred home sites) to market. Appreciation events recognized individual Realtors or Realtor offices for their accomplishments (typically number of homes sold in the community or dollar volume of sales in a year). Most or our events involved a business presentation of some form (information on the homes or neighborhood, for example) tied in with a social event (dinner or cocktail reception and usually some form of entertainment).

Our events were usually packed and oversubscribed. Realtors clamored for an invitation. When

I asked Dick what his formula for success was, he put it succinctly: "You can never have too many jumbo shrimp at a broker event."

The more I have pondered this statement, the truer it became. The essence was that Dick knew what his target market valued (food) and he knew that jumbo shrimp were the highest value coin of the realm for that market. If you had great jumbo shrimp, it said that you cared enough about your guests to make sure you had what they loved. You cared about them. You also did not try to cut corners. They knew if the shrimp was not the best (Realtor attendance at many events gave them a true critic's appreciation of top quality and that which was "off," even by a little). You also did not want to run out, either, because it put a damper on the event and sent a message that either you did not plan well or that you might be cash strapped. These were not good brand images.

You could have a so-so cheese tray and get away with it. Nobody judged you and your organization by your raw vegetables and dip, either. But they came to the event for the jumbo shrimp and the knowledge that you always had the best and had a bottomless pit of supply. It was the gold standard for them.

The more they came to Dick's events, the more houses we sold. The more houses we sold, the more money we made. The more houses that Realtors sold, the more commission income they earned. It was an absolutely virtuous circle of a relationship.

Dick's simple phrase embodied the lesson that you have to know what your market wants and values, and then deliver it flawlessly. If you can't do that, don't do it at all.

### *"You can never have too many jumbo shrimp at a broker event."*

Exercise: Are there some rules of thumb that you would use to impart learned truths about marketing or promotion in your business? What would they be?

_____

_____

_____

_____

_____

_____

_____

_____

_____

_____

_____

_____

_____

_____

_____

_____

_____

_____

_____

_____

_____

# 5

## SKINNY KIDS

*Sales are the lifeblood of any business, yet sometimes managers forget that fact, potentially putting all employees at risk. There are some observations and best practices that might help to ensure that your sales stay up to par.*

I have the utmost respect for those individuals who sell things, particularly on a commission basis. I have often used the expression "No Sell; No Eat" to describe the absolutely Darwinian nature of the profession, both on the individual and on an organization.

It is the last vestige of the true hunter-gatherer, our prehistoric ancestors who daily had to hunt for food. If they succeeded, the individual and family had sustenance for another day or two. If they failed, they were one step closer to death.

In our "civilized" society, this cycle plays itself out in subtle, organizational ways. We have sales departments, marketing departments, accounting departments, finance departments, production departments, legal departments, and so forth that spread the effort of the business of trying to make and sell things that have higher value than their costs. However, when you get down to it, the absolute critical link in the chain is those charged with selling the product. If they succeed, there is revenue to help cover the costs of making and selling the product. If they fail, no matter how good the other departments are, there is no revenue or insufficient revenue and the whole organization begins to atrophy.

Despite the life-or-death nature and importance of selling, it has amazed me how cavalier many managers are about their sales staff. In order to succeed as a salesperson, there is this critical balance between rejection and fear of rejection and optimism about being able to succeed. Training is critical. Psychological management is even more critical. So is being there at the point of sale. I can't tell you how many times I have walked into a builder's sales office or to the parts counter of an auto supply store and there is no one there.

The first rule of selling is that you have to be there when someone wants to buy. I don't care how good the product is or how good the value is or how successfully the product has created buzz in the marketplace. If no one is there to interface with a customer, the sale will not happen and the whole organization is in jeopardy.

Similarly, I have been amazed at how uninvolved many managers are in the process of screening, hiring, and training their salespeople. Enough work has been done to know that there are certain psychological profiles that are possessed by successful salespeople and that certain training regimens and processes create a higher probability of a sale than no process at all. Nothing is certain, but the odds favor those who screen for the right people, train them well, and put them into a good system. This, coupled with good management, gives at least fertile soil for the generation of revenue and prosperity for the organization.

My longtime friend and mentor, Martin Freedland of the Berke Group in Atlanta, has studied, consulted upon, and taught in this area for decades. He was able to take this lesson and pass it on succinctly in a memorable phrase: "Shy salespeople have skinny kids," which has long been attributed to sales guru Zig Ziglar.

The phrase captures the truth that salespeople need to have the core psychological attributes for selling (an outgoing personality being only one key ingredient). By ignoring those key ingredients, the "kids," whether they be the biological offspring of the salesperson or those in the organization who depend on the revenue that the salesperson generates, will be less well off, and that is not good for anyone. The solution is a disciplined approach to hiring, training, managing, and compensating salespeople.

I have had the pleasure and agony of having both great and awful salespeople work for me.

One of my first, Jim Sullivan, had the voice of a radio announcer and was the sales manager at Toll Brothers' Yardley Hunt community in Yardley, Pennsylvania, about halfway between Philadelphia and New York City. At six foot two, he was imposing, but had the drill down when it came to selling homes. He baked homemade bread and chocolate chip cookies in the kitchen of the model home every Sunday to create the "homey" smell that was conducive to selling houses. He listened to what customers wanted and figured out how he could help them. He followed up on questions with regular return calls. He always had his list of "top ten" prospects that he worked. After people bought and moved in, he stopped by to see how they were doing and brought them small gifts to thank them for buying from him.

They loved him and brought him more leads.

Jim sold ninety homes per year at a time when thirty a year was considered a lot. He did nearly everything that a good salesperson should do and loved doing it. He prospered and, as a company, we did also. Our sales were always the best in the area and our profitability was high. It was perfect.

But, contrast that to the sales representative for a local Phoenix area builder that I encountered a couple of years ago, just as the new home market had started its precipitous drop. The builder was one of about ten in DMB's huge Phoenix-area master planned community, Verrado®, where I was the general manager. For nearly a decade, new home sales in the Phoenix marketplace had been like shooting fish in a barrel. You didn't have to be good at selling in order to have great sales. People bought in spite of themselves out of greed or fear of losing out on a good deal. Great sales came from just being open in the right locations.

When the market started to decline in 2007, sales were harder to make, and the old-school disciplines of having clean models and a professional and trained sales manager were more important than ever.

One Sunday, my wife and I walked into one builder's model home in Verrado to check things out. (I was interested in the builder's sales because if he sold his houses, he would need more lots from us. We were a step back in the chain from his retail store.) My wife and I hit his "target market": empty-nest couples. We walked into the sales office and he was speaking with someone. We spent about five minutes walking around the sales office looking at displays and information. Not once did he recognize our presence, either verbally or with just a look. We were invisible. After five minutes, we took it upon ourselves to just walk the model homes ourselves, which took about twenty minutes.

In the models, there were blown-out light bulbs, unkempt furniture, and the cleaning was marginal. Not an enticing retail experience. After the twenty minutes, we returned to the sales office, and the sales manager was still speaking with the same person. Again, we waited about five minutes, anticipating some kind of acknowledgement, which did not come, so, we walked out the door without ever making any kind of connection.

Next door was another builder's model home, so we went in there, too. The saleswoman was speaking with someone on the telephone, but we heard her say immediately, "Excuse me. Some customers just came in." She then quickly said hello to us, explained that she was speaking with another customer who had purchased, and invited us to walk the models, saying that she would catch up with us when we returned. It was professional to both us and the customer on the phone.

When we returned, she offered us a bottle of water, inquired about us and what we might be looking for, and did a great job just establishing a pleasant and professional rapport with us.

It was no surprise that the first builder was complaining that he was not making any sales in our community and wanted to know what we were going to do to increase advertising, because his reported traffic was down and he was not making anywhere close to his sales plan. The second builder, although his traffic and sales were down from the previous year, still was selling at a reasonable pace.

When I reported my experience to the first builder, he was in denial: "That is my best salesperson. He has been with me five years and always sold before. It can't be him." Needless to say, the builder did not change anything (he visited the sales office only two days per month) and within a year he defaulted on his bank loans, and he ultimately went bankrupt. The second builder has managed to ride out the downturn and is surviving.

The point is very simple, though. The tougher the environment, the more important sales become, and the more critical the right choice for salespeople becomes. It doesn't hurt for managers to be at the point of sale more frequently, either, just to see how the sales force is performing and to learn what might be done better.

The kids are depending on it.

## *"Shy salespeople have skinny kids."*

Exercise: Are there lessons that you have learned about selling? Can you boil them down to some simple nuggets of wisdom? What are they?

_____

_____

_____

_____

_____

_____

_____

_____

_____

_____

_____

_____

_____

_____

_____

_____

_____

_____

_____

_____

_____

_____

# 6

## HALF A LOAF

*Throughout business, negotiations happen every day and at every level of an organization. Knowing your relative bargaining power in the current business environment is crucial for having a successful negotiation. Here are some thoughts in that regard.*

Negotiation is the very heart of business. When we buy, when we sell, when we hire, when we fire, when we change, when we don't change: they all involve negotiation. By its nature, negotiation involves ego, relative power, and ultimately the willingness to compromise. These factors play out against each other time after time.

For much of my career, I have been involved in the homebuilding business. As one of the highest-cost items retail purchasers acquire in their lifetime, homes are a treacherous item when they involve negotiation. The buyer has the emotions of long-term economics, family security, and desire for neighborhood and the image that neighborhood portrays to consider. The builder has to weigh immense cost, time, and labor invested in a mostly irreplaceable asset. In hot markets the builder has the relative upper hand, and in slow markets the buyer does. In all cases, emotions and egos can run hot.

From a business standpoint, the most difficult time is the slow market, when supply exceeds demand and values may be dropping week after week while costs are not. Margins erode and cash flow becomes critical.

As a newly minted MBA in the mid-1970s, I knew the theory of how to handle these situations more than I had experienced the practice. In the housing downturn of the late 1970s and early 1980s, I was a project manager for Toll Brothers building homes in Yardley, Pennsylvania, and Lawrenceville, New Jersey, both communities hugging the Delaware River, about halfway between New York and Philadelphia. My superintendent at the time, Tom Maloney, was a carpenter by trade and was blessed with wisdom far beyond his years and relative life exposure. In negotiating the sale of houses in this slow time, Tom would use the expression "Half a loaf is better than no loaf at all" when we were faced with an offer that was less than what we wanted. His counsel was that getting another house off the books, another family in a home in the community, and cash back into the bank account that we could put to work again was a better outcome than stubbornly holding out for a higher price or better terms.

Since that time, the advice has almost always held true. Something is almost always better than nothing. It gives you the opportunity to live to another day. It gives you a data point on what the real market is willing to pay at a point in time, and that intelligence can help you retool your product, renegotiate your costs, or adjust your overhead in order to remain profitable in the "new" market.

"Half a loaf" is often coupled with "sooner is better than later" and "never charge less than what the market will bear." Figuring out what the market will bear at a point in time is both an art and a science and is subject to constant testing and evaluation. The faster it is done, the more feedback you get in order to adjust. The willingness to get something (half a loaf) rather than nothing (no loaf at all) is the psychological grease that allows this to occur.

In the wind-down of the bubble housing market in 2005-2008, I was amazed at how many builders held their prices in the face of week after week of no sales and climbing inventories. After several hot years, there was a cultural unwillingness to bend and adapt to a new market where suddenly the buyer, rather than the seller, held the upper hand. Those who did adapt and moved their inventory at whatever price the market would bear that day not only reduced their inventory exposure, but they also had the opportunity to adjust their product and pricing offerings based on their recent experience. It may not have been pretty, but it reflected reality.

In early 2008, one of the private, high-end production builders at our Verrado master planned community in Buckeye, Arizona, had seen his sales go dead as the market had gone into full retreat. He was sitting on over thirty finished "spec" homes, and his sales had been zero for several straight months. He had stubbornly held to his pricing (in part to stay in conformance with his bank loan covenants), while some of the public builders in the community had been reducing their pricing and/or increasing their incentives in order to make sales happen, albeit at lower paces than they had previously enjoyed.

Finally, the high-end builder announced in late-January 2008 that he had engaged an auction company to have a one-day auction of all of his spec homes. For the next month, sales for all of our builders dropped to near zero, as there was uncertainty about what the pricing on the auction homes would be and how that would impact the pricing and value of the other builders' homes.

On the day of the auction, all of the spec homes were sold and the prices, although considerably less than the pricing the builder had on the homes originally, were consistent on a price-per-square-foot basis to the pricing the public builders had been getting on their homes prior to the announcement of the auction. Once the auction occurred and the market saw that the pricing in the community had been validated, all of the builders began to sell at levels that were higher than before.

By being willing to take "half a loaf," the high-end builder (and his bank) both validated a pricing level and converted his assets into cash very quickly. In retrospect, it was a great move. In the summer of 2008, the mortgage market really blew up, and the credit crunch hit with full force. Pricing for all homes dropped another 20 percent or more over the next nine months, and, as of the end of 2009, had not returned to the levels achieved in the auction of February 2008. Builders (and lenders) who continued to adjust to the market, even as it kept falling, ended up getting more return than those who tried to wait the market out.

The observation goes back centuries. It can be found in the text of *Don Quixote* and in medieval English writing, to name a few. But it is a truism that has to be respected and remembered by managers, particularly in slow times. I thank Tom Maloney for teaching it to me.

*"Half a loaf is better than no loaf at all."*

Exercise: Are there some rules or lessons that you have regarding negotiations? What would they be?

_____

_____

_____

_____

_____

_____

_____

_____

_____

_____

_____

_____

_____

_____

_____

_____

_____

_____

# 7

## FEEDING GOATS

*Advertising is a confounding medium, yet it is essential for most businesses. When a manager is facing a decision whether to advertise or how much to spend on advertising, remembering a simple farm animal can help.*

Timing is a kind of luck that you can control, to some extent. Having a sense of the market and one's relative market power, as we saw in "Half a Loaf," is important. Being actually "in" the market, as opposed to just observing a market from the sidelines, provides real-time information for an adept manager to be able to make decisions. In his song "The Gambler," Kenny Rogers advises: "Know when to hold 'em, know when to fold 'em; know when to walk away, know when to run."

Experience helps to hone the sixth sense of when to do what.

One of the toughest cost centers to deal with for a company is advertising and promotion. It is a chicken-and-egg world. If you don't advertise, you might not get sales and the "kids" might get skinny. On the other hand, you never quite know whether your advertising is worth what you are paying for it, and you might be pouring money down the drain for no good benefit. Adding to the uncertainty is the fact that you only have a sense as to whether advertising and promotion expenses are working *after* the commitment to spend and the execution of the program have occurred.

How does a manager strike a balance?

Early in my career, Bob Toll used an expression that seemed to handle the situation. He said: "Put the hay down when the goats can get it."

Bob was usually aggressive in advertising and promotion, but he had a fine nose for the onset of a slump and a diminution of demand. When exogenous events (national recessions, freeze-ups in credit markets, etc.) happen, trying to spur demand by advertising really has to be thought through, because, most often, the money is wasted and does not spur demand at all.

If people are scared, they don't buy. If financing isn't there, they can't buy. If social pressure around customers frowns on buying, purchases are deferred.

Turning off the "advertising machine" in a company can be a painful process. There are people in the organization and outside of it whose jobs are tied to developing and executing marketing plans and events. There are vendors, suppliers, media outlets, consultants, and others whose livelihoods depend on the flow of money in advertising and promotional campaigns. When a company looks at slowing or stopping the flow, there are more than a few oxen to be gored in the process. On the other hand, if the manager's responsibility is to ensure that capital is being used wisely, throwing money at a market that is not there is surely a colossal waste.

In 2008, as the national housing downturn had really taken hold, builders and developers who advertised strongly did not have significantly better results compared to those who had trimmed back advertising significantly or eliminated it all together. If people wanted to buy or had to buy, they did.

At the Verrado community in Arizona, homebuilder sales office traffic that actually purchased homes rose from slightly over 1 percent to over 2 percent. Even though absolute sales dropped (because the overall traffic had declined), it showed that the people coming in the door consisted of more "potential buyers" and fewer "tire kickers." The smartest of the builders reduced their marketing budgets proportionately with their sales declines and seemed to always be experimenting with various media and messages to see what worked. It was a lot of work.

Not putting the hay down doesn't mean that advertising has to go to zero. Low-cost outreach efforts via the Web, Twitter, and other low-cost media can help keep a brand presence and may be highly cost effective. However, running the big multimedia ad campaign into the face of an economic storm probably is not a good use of funds.

The smartest operators knew the historic ratio of advertising expense to sales revenue (in the building business it is usually 1 percent) and kept adjusting their budgets to their best guess of both unit sales and revenues on a frequent (monthly) basis. If revenues were declining, they adjusted their budget downward and then tried to figure out how to get the most "bang" out of what budget did remain.

In other industries, the same logic would apply by applying the classical advertising percentage to anticipated revenues and then testing and adjusting frequently.

The lesson can also apply in good times, but in a slightly different variation.

Sometimes people will buy in sufficient quantity that advertising is not needed at all. In the final years of Weston, in South Florida, from 1999 to 2002, we had a well-established brand for our community and had worked a very strong broker outreach program. Starting in 1999, we began to trim our traditional print and broadcast media exposure back to see what impact the decrease had on sales. It was negligible, so by the time we got into 2000, we were just focusing on our Web presence, broker outreach, and community programming efforts.

Based on the previous ratios of advertising to revenues, we were trimming out about $4 million per year in advertising and related expense, without impacting our sales level appreciably. It took guts to make that experiment and to follow the facts, but in the final three years of the community, over $10 million that would have normally just flowed into advertising and promotion flowed to the bottom line instead.

Like all things in management, whether "the goats are eating" changes with time and is best determined by reasoned experimentation. Keep testing the market with small efforts to see if conditions have changed. The more treacherous the market, the more frequent the evaluation and adjustments have to be. If some additional advertising seems to be cost effective in spurring demand and profitability, then try more. If it doesn't, try trimming back to see if reducing expenditures has any impact on demand or profitability.

By constantly doing this exercise, the balance between cost savings and wise investment in marketing can be attained, the "goats" will be correctly fed, and your wallet will not be unduly emptied.

## *"Put the hay down when the goats can get it."*

Exercise: What are the lessons that you have learned about advertising? How would you state each in a simple and memorable phrase or two?

_____

_____

_____

_____

_____

_____

_____

_____

_____

_____

_____

_____

_____

_____

_____

_____

_____

_____

_____

_____

_____

# 8

## GOOD INFORMATION

*Does it seem like your job is controlling you, rather than you controlling your job? Are employees or co-workers lobbying you to make a decision and you are not quite sure how to make the call? Learning how to obtain the data you need and then to use that data to make improvements or decisions is a key skill to develop as a manager. Words from an American who was the godfather of the Japanese quality movement can help remind you of this basic and important lesson.*

I first became aware of the Total Quality Management (TQM) movement in the early 1990s. It was a time when U.S. manufacturing was struggling, and it seemed like Japanese firms were going to take over the world. Toyota was waxing the U.S. automakers and Sony was introducing category-killers like the Walkman and Discman®. Not only did the Japanese companies have better products with better designs, but their cost structures were just plain better, primarily because they were more efficient in their production and had fewer defects. *Kaizen*, the Japanese philosophy of continuous improvement, started to work into the lexicon of business as American companies began to try to catch up.

I took courses in TQM at the Penn State Extension outside of Philadelphia in the early 1990s and, later, a comprehensive series of courses from the Center for Quality Management in Cincinnati in the mid-1990s. General Electric had begun to develop its group of "Six Sigma Black Belts" who would attack process improvement projects in the company, and that was helping to differentiate GE from other U.S. manufacturers. I was lucky enough to have some of these folks in my Cincinnati classes, and it proved to me that a Japanese-style system for quality and improvement could be introduced successfully into an American company. It just took hard work.

Having been in homebuilding at this point for more than ten years, I was all too aware of the multiple problems in the homebuilding process and the costs of those problems. I would wake up in sweats at night worrying about "what if Toyota announced tomorrow that it was entering the U.S. homebuilding industry with a business model based on its auto manufacturing?" I knew that nearly 100% of homebuilders in the United States would be out of business. If that was a fate I did not desire, I felt that I had to learn about TQM, kaizen, and any other methods of doing things better in order to have a leg up on my competitors and have a chance for survival.

What surprised me, as I began studying TQM, was that its Japanese roots actually came from an American, W. Edwards Deming. Deming taught the basics of statistical analysis to industrial companies in post-World War II Japan. Deming's fourteen points became the basis of the business philosophy of Japan's best industrial companies, in part because Deming's philosophy of continuous improvement meshed well with major pieces of Japanese culture. Deming became a hero in Japan but was nearly an unknown in the United States.

Deep in the heart of Deming's work was the importance of gathering data and learning to interpret the data to learn how a process was working and then to make changes to see if relevant measures of the process got better. Done over and over again, the result was a culture of taking every piece of what an organization did and trying to make it both simple and defect free. Simple operations tended to take less time to do and led to higher productivity (and lower costs). Eliminating defects cut waste, improved productivity, and lowered costs, too. These were all good things in competitive industries.

A simple quote attributed to Deming—"In God we trust; all others bring data"—was easy to remember and seemed to sum up a core element of the philosophy: let the data speak to you without bias, and trust the data to lead you to improvement or to make a decision.

Having the right data helped to improve the chance of a "good" decision. Data is apolitical and impersonal and provides a good jumping-off place for decisions and change.

Almost immediately, I began to implement Deming's ideas and to teach them to my middle managers in a non-intimidating way. I had learned that TQM was a foreign concept to many in the business, but the idea of making things better was pretty simple to grasp, and most people could sign on to that idea pretty easily.

The concept of TQM had developed a negative connotation in some companies by the mid-1990s. In many companies it denoted a lot of "touchy-feely" team exercises with everyone having to learn about statistics. Whole new corporate departments were being created to try to teach everyone the basics. The "structure" of TQM was overtaking the actual simple things that made TQM work to the point that people didn't want to take on anything associated with the quality movement, because it looked like a giant black hole of expense that did not justify the outcomes.

For every company that was a success story in the Malcolm Baldrige Awards (the annual recognition awards for success in application of Total Quality Management), there seemed to be more stories of failure, abandonment, and frustration. It seemed, though, that the companies that took more simple approaches and tended to leave the word "quality" out of the lexicon seemed to do better.

General Electric seemed to have the better idea. It taught a small group of specialists the techniques of TQM and then imbedded them with day-to-day workers and managers to work on projects until a change was implemented. The line workers had an input and involvement with the change, but did not have to deal with multiple courses and statistics. That was for the "Black Belts" who would do the process over and over again and became very good at it.

While building Arvida's Weston community, just west of Fort Lauderdale, in the late 1990s and early 2000s, we were building over twelve hundred homes per year. At the time, the company had already built over ten thousand homes in the community (dating back to 1984), and the management of customer warranty service was a huge task. Bill Frey, the director of warranty service at the time at Weston, prided himself as a can-do "firefighter" who would just bull his way through issues and get them resolved, even if the same types of issues occurred over and over again, year after year. He had nearly thirty people in his department handling phones, going out on service calls, and managing subcontractor appointments back into customer homes.

If there was any data tracking, it was pretty rudimentary. He did not have good data on how many service orders were outstanding, how long each had been outstanding, how that data broke down by subcontractor, or how it broke down by types of service call issue. Everyone was working as fast and as hard as he or she could, but never seemed to get ahead. It was pure chaos.

With the help of two of my trusted senior managers who "got" the idea of TQM, Rich Rodriguez and Bill Petkoski, and a consultant, Lee Harkins, who had been involved with TQM efforts at Bell South, we began to teach Bill how to gather data, how to analyze it to find defect patterns, and then how to attack those problems. It wasn't fancy and it wasn't called TQM. It was just teaching Bill and his people a different way of managing.

First, we hired someone whose sole job was to develop an accurate database so that we could begin to manage the service information. That effort took nearly three months to get up and running, but once it did, it provided the raw data we could begin to work with. For example, we saw that the average time to complete a customer's service request was thirty-two days, but it was not uncommon to have service items outstanding for over 180 days. That was not good. We also began to see, by trade partner, who had how many service tickets outstanding and how long it took to get them resolved.

For example, we saw that the heating and air-conditioning subcontractor almost always had its service tickets resolved within a week of a customer's notice of a problem, and rarely was there something older than a month. On the other hand, the plumber rarely had work done inside of two weeks, and most of the tickets were older than a month.

As we started to ask why, the answers began to jump off the computer printout. The heating and air-conditioning contractor not only had organized himself to do new home construction, he had also organized a very efficient service department, knowing that service on the nearly 16,000 homes in our community (at build-out) would be an ongoing cash cow for him for years if he worked at building his service business.

On the other hand, the plumber had no desire to be in the service business. He just wanted to do the new home construction. His pricing for that work was great, and that was why he was awarded the work. However, in the contracting process, standards for service performance had been nearly totally ignored, and there was no real penalty for lax service perform-ance. In the structure of the purchasing, price was given a much higher priority than service.

After learning this, we quickly began to renegotiate our contracts to include a service performance provi-sion. In the case of the plumber (and others), if they did not meet the performance standard, we had the right to go to another vendor to do the service work. If it was warranty work that was the responsibility of the plumber, we would back-charge him for the work at the cost of the other plumber brought in to do the work. If the work was not the original plumber's responsibility (for example, a toilet having to be removed and reset because of a tile problem), he just did not get the incremental work, and the other plumber did.

Since nearly half of the service work was not a direct warranty problem for the plumber, we found that using a plumber who did want to be in the service business for the long term sped the process up. When there was true warranty work for the original plumber, he actually did a better job of doing the work quickly, because he did not want to be back-charged for the work by another (higher-rate) plumber. The end result was that the response times for plumbing service calls got better and our costs did not climb, primarily because we had read the data and decided to try some changes.

Bill, tentatively at first, began to gather data on other service calls and to look at the data, too. His "ah-ha" moment came when he found that the highest frequency of service calls was for electrical items. Going deeper into the data, he found that the highest-frequency electrical item was for defective doorbells. As he dug deeper, he found that nearly a quarter of the doorbells installed by the electrician were defective, primarily due to a defect in the "button" at the front door.

With the help of Lee Harkins, they determined that the button the electrician was using cost a small amount, something like 25 cents, but that the cost of a service call was nearly $50. By shifting to a slightly better "button" that cost a few cents more, the warranty issue disappeared. Convincing the electrical subcontractor to move to the more expensive button was easy, because Bill had the data on frequency of defect, cost of repair, and the net benefit to the electrician's bottom line. By the way, he now had fewer defects to manage and could go concentrate on other ones, picking them off easily with the skill set he had developed.

With that experience in hand, Bill became a maniac on data and a phenomenal warranty manager, too. He had learned the power of data to help him improve his department, cut costs, improve customer satisfaction, and to bring order to what had been a disorderly world. If you were to find Bill today and ask him, he would readily admit that learning to gather and trust data in helping him manage was one of the best things he ever learned as a manager.

And, by the way, on his office was a large, printed sign that said to all who viewed it:

*"In God we trust; all others bring data."*

Exercise: What are the three most important pieces of data that you have to have to do your job? Why? If you could have a fourth, what would it be and why?

_____

_____

_____

_____

_____

_____

_____

_____

_____

_____

_____

_____

_____

_____

_____

_____

_____

_____

_____

_____

_____

_____

# 9

## BEER AND CHANGE

*Changing how things are done can be one of the most frustrating under-takings for a manager. The bigger the change, it seems, the harder it is. Yet managers have to drive change to respond to market conditions and to survive as an enterprise. Respecting the advice of Albert Einstein and the lessons learned from a game about distributing beer can help you recall the key elements for a successful change.*

As part of my exploration into the world of Total Quality Management and process improvement and how those ideas could help make homebuilding and development operations better, I became aware of a day program at the Massachusetts Institute of Technology (MIT) in something called "System Dynamics."

As described in Wikipedia:

"System Dynamics is a powerful methodology and computer simulation modeling technique for framing, understanding, and discussing complex issues and problems. Originally developed in the 1950s to help corporate managers improve their understanding of industrial processes, system dynamics is currently being used throughout the public and private sector for policy analysis and design.

"System Dynamics is an aspect of systems theory and is a method for understanding the dynamic behavior of complex systems. The basis of the method is the recognition that the structure of any system—the many circular, interlocking, some-times time-delayed relationships among its components—is often just as important in determining its behavior as the individual components themselves. Examples are chaos theory and social dynamics. It is also claimed that because there are often properties-of-the-whole, which cannot be found among the properties-of-the-elements, in some cases the behavior of the whole cannot be explained in terms of the behavior of the parts."

For an engineer with an MBA, this was good stuff.

I hoped that an exposure to System Dynamics would help me advance the work I had been doing in trying to bring process control and improvement strategies to the problem of building and servicing large numbers of homes simultaneously with higher quality and faster cycle times.

At the Weston community in South Florida, we had over seven hundred homes under construction at any one time, and I was beginning to hit a wall on my efforts to reduce the time it took to build a home and to improve the quality at the same time. We had over ten thousand homes that had been built in the community, and part of my responsibility was to build the remaining six thousand homes in less than five years. To do this required a pace of production at least

25 percent greater than the organization had ever done.

The MIT System Dynamics class that I attended was an international one consisting of about one hundred managers from multiple countries and industries. I was not surprised when the director of the program noted that I was, to his knowledge, one of only a handful of executives from the homebuilding/real estate development industry that had ever attended the course over a period of several decades. It was just another indicator that there was low hanging fruit on homebuilding's competitive landscape to be picked.

As part of the program, we got to spend an afternoon playing a game called "the Beer Game," where tables of eight players run a simulated beer production and distribution system. Some run a retail store that has to respond to customer demand for beer (driven by supposedly random cards drawn from a deck). Based on what they see in terms of demand, they have to order replacement beer supply from their wholesaler who, in turn, has to order from a distributor, who has to order it from the brewery. You gain profits by selling cases of beer to the next person in the chain, but, at the end of the game, each step in the chain is penalized for the number of cases in inventory that are left. Teams are also penalized for instances when there is demand, but you are "out of stock" during the game. Teams become very competitive in the game and try various strategies to maximize profits.

At the end, each team posts its scores and inventory levels. That data are then compared and then tested against the data from previous classes from prior months and years. What becomes stunningly obvious is that the range of results is remarkably tight over a long period of time. There are winners and losers in each session, but when charted over time, the range of results becomes very predictable and very consistent.

It didn't matter whether it was a group of scientists from NASA or a group of nuns from a hospital in the Midwest, everyone's results were driven by the rules and structure of the game. As smart as you might be, you couldn't change the results markedly. The "system" was really the primary determinant of what the result was going to be. The intelligence, experience, or level of sophistication of the participants had only a minor impact on results compared to the structure and rules of the system.

Albert Einstein is credited with the quote: "The definition of insanity is doing the same thing over and over again and expecting different results." It seemed to apply to this game in spades. With decades of testing and leaving the core system in place, the results were all "the same" (that is, within a very narrow band of outcomes).

In a later playing of the Beer Game, we were allowed to change one element of the game rules that significantly reduced the time delay between a need at the retail store and the brewing of a batch of beer to satisfy the retail store's need (kind of a simplified version of Walmart's daily linking of sales information back to its manufacturers, so that they can more quickly see what is selling and prepare to refill fast-selling items).

Sure enough, when the game was played again under the new rules, the results were significantly different. Although still covering a range of outcomes, the overall range was much more profitable than the range from the previous rules. Only by changing the structure and rules of the game did we end up with a truly different (and better) result.

The simplified lesson from this was that systems and structures primarily determine outcomes and that the influence of individual factors (intelligence, perseverance, etc.) was secondary, although still measurable.

Put more simply, putting ordinary people in a superb system oftentimes gave better results than putting extraordinary people into a deficient system. However, putting extraordinary people into a great system usually gave better results than results from ordinary people. Since finding teams of extraordinary people is both hard and fragile, the takeaway was that changing the structure and systems was the more certain way of getting better results over the long term.

One of my first trials of the "new system" approach was in the area of attaining building permits for the Weston community. We had a staff of around five at Weston who processed the building permits for the houses we had sold and needed to build and then delivered that permit package to the Broward County Building office for its processing.

Once a house had been sold, the project manager for that house line would tell the Permit Group that the house needed to be permitted. This was typically in the form of a notice to proceed. The group would then set about collecting all of the drawings, site maps, certificates of water and sewer availability, and other documents needed to submit the permit package to the City of Weston for zoning review.

When that was approved by the City, the package would then be carried to the building department for Broward County in Fort Lauderdale, about forty minutes away, which would then review the entire package and, usually after several rejections for various missing items or questionable calls, the permit would be issued and construction could start.

The process was complicated by the fact that the county building department had over two dozen permit reviewers, and each had a slightly different set of standards it used to accept or reject a permit application. A building permit package for one house would pass one reviewer, but would be rejected by another for the same reason and then rejected by a third on another review for a separate set of reasons.

There was no certainty that the initial reviewer of a package would do the re-review of the corrected and amended package when it came back in again. Needless to say, it took anywhere from thirty to 120 days to actually get a building permit, and there were multiple cases of one permit being submitted months after another, yet coming out sooner. Buyers, who were trying to make their life plans around when their house would be started and finished, were obviously distressed by this randomness, as were our salespeople and project managers.

Chaos was the only way to describe the process, and yelling and finger pointing were common events.

The head of the building department, Coz Tornice, a practical manager who did not like the results, either, was open to ideas for a better and different way. Luckily, our community was a major contributor to both his workload and his revenue stream.

The first thing we did was agree that we wanted a better result: fewer rejections, faster turnaround times, less stress for all. We then started a process of weekly meetings to review the status of all the permit applications we had in and to find common causes of rejection that we could work on correcting systemically. Most important, we sold him on the idea of even flow. We told him that we were on a plan for twenty-five starts a week, and as long as we could get twenty-five permits a week, we were fine. We also knew both when houses were sold and what customers had critical delivery dates and which ones had flexibility. By consolidating this information weekly at our office, our representative could sit with the building department staff and work on which permits could come out in what order and then focus on what it took to get those twenty-five out for that week.

After about a month, things started to work better. There was an order to the process that developed. The building department agreed to have applications sit with the same reviewer all of the way through review. We began to develop a list of major inconsistencies of interpretation between reviewers so that Coz could work on those items. (He had never known of the chaos caused by the nuances of different interpretations by his reviewers.)

With consistency of interpretation, we developed a tighter checklist of items that had to be completed before we submitted a permit package, knowing that if we got it right, the rejections would have to drop, rework would go down, and permits could come out faster.

The reviewers appreciated the orderliness and predictability of the process. They could organize to be able to make sure that we got our twenty-five permits per week and didn't have to worry about high degrees of variability they got from other builders. First slowly, then more quickly, the turnaround times dropped to the point that it was taking about three weeks to get a permit, and the variance around that time was not large.

The days of the 120-plus day time frame to get a permit drifted into the past. We now could give a higher degree of certainty to our customers on when their homes could start, once their building permit had been submitted.

Changing the system and structure had changed the outcome remarkably, even though the people involved had remained exactly the same.

Now that was a game changer that one could toast with a glass of beer.

*"By doing what you have always done, you, most likely, will continue to get what you have always gotten. Only by changing systems and structures can you get sustainable, long-term, better results."*

Exercise: What was a change project that went well, and what was one that did not? Why did they succeed or fail? After reading this chapter, what would you do differently, if anything?

_____

_____

_____

_____

_____

_____

_____

_____

_____

_____

_____

_____

_____

_____

_____

_____

_____

_____

_____

# 10

## ORGANIZATIONS

*Are you having a tough time getting a set of changes or improvements implemented? Changing the systems that you use and the policies you have can only go so far. Sometimes a deeper change is needed in order to make the smaller changes work: a change to the fundamental organization of the company or division.*

The enlightenment from the MIT System Dynamics course that, in order to get a different result, you needed a different system, took a while to set in. But its implications had been rumbling inside of my head even before the course; albeit in an amorphous manner.

Since the mid 1980s I had begun to wonder why organizations did what they did, and why some did things better than others. In the world of homebuilding, a typical organization would have a president, a head of construction operations (which would include both the construction in the field and the back office that did purchasing and estimating and warranty work), a head of sales and marketing, sometimes an in-house lawyer or a head of human resources or an office manager, and a head of finance and accounting. Sometimes the construction operations task was split in two, sometimes sales and marketing were split, and sometimes finance and accounting were split. These decisions were driven more by the skill set of individuals than by the necessary tasks that needed to be done.

People tended to grow up in a particular skill set, and rarely did skill sets cross. A head of construction who had come up through marketing or sales or vice versa was a true needle-in-the-haystack. The organizational interfaces between departments developed over time and were a function of both the personalities involved and the natural frictions that occur when the world of one function bumps up against the world of another.

The policies of the company developed as a result of those frictions and the lessons learned from the frictions. If improvements occurred, they tended to be within a function (for example, paying bills more quickly or handling customer service requests more quickly).

Improvements that had impacts across multiple departments and benefitted the entire organization's performance were much more difficult to achieve, as they required the focused effort of the top leader (usually the CEO or the president) to implement the change. The top executive usually was the only person who had authority across all of the departments and could drive such a cross-departmental change agenda. The larger the organization, the harder it was.

Functionally organized companies tended to do their functional work well, but any task that involved constant multifunctional management was difficult.

From a succession standpoint, functional organizations had a difficult time developing generalist managers who saw the breadth of the organization and its strategy. Typically those from the legal and financial functions were the only ones able to see this breadth, and they became the easiest people to move into senior management, sometimes to the detriment of the company, because they often did not have a true depth of operational experience in the business itself.

Think of the promotions to chief executive officer at the big automobile companies that came from those in the chief financial officer role (rather than "car guys") or those at the big banks that came from the CFO or general counsel role (rather than "banking guys"). Even though they had the "top level view" of the company, one has to wonder whether they truly understood how the operating business really worked. Ultimately, that lack of understanding of the true value generation element of the company may have been an inhibitor in their ability to truly manage the company in turbulent times.

With very few generalists, functionally organized companies had a difficult time expanding to other geographic areas. There just were not enough people who understood all of the aspects of the business. Companies who did attempt to expand by trying to use functional specialists oftentimes came to grief in the new market.

In the late 1970s, Toll Brothers became one of the few homebuilders to abandon the classic functional organization and to adopt a project management structure instead. Project managers were intended to be generalists from the start. They were responsible for the land acquisition, development, construction, purchasing, warranty, sales, marketing, and financial performance of their project or projects.

Project managers came from all kinds of backgrounds. Some were up-from-the-ranks superintendents, some were engineers, some were lawyers, some were architects, some were marketing and sales types, some were accountants or financial analysts, and some were from pure liberal arts backgrounds. Although they did not necessarily possess the technical skills that resided in a functional organization, they were more adept at working quickly for the benefit of the project in its individual environment of competition, politics, and customers.

Those who could learn quickly ("It is a wise man who knows what he does not know") from their functional experts and from their environment and then convert that learning into profitable strategies became the winners. Good project managers grew up to easily train and manage other project managers, and an organization that grew generalist managers resulted.

After ten years at Toll as its first project manager and one of its senior leaders, I left to grow into a senior management/chief financial officer position at a competitor. At that time, through contact with many other builders on a national basis who had functional organizations, I started to wonder: which organizational structure produced better results.

Study and analysis seemed to indicate that the functionally organized companies tended to do their functions better than Toll or other project-management-based organizations, on the whole. Toll, on the other hand, seemed to handle its growth from being a regional player in Pennsylvania and New Jersey to a national player from the early 1980s through the late 1990s much better than its competitors.

That began to make sense. The organization was very good at developing generalist managers, which were critical to the expansion. It lost the functional consistency that the other builders had, because each project manager had latitude in adaptation to his or her management style and environment, but the organizational benefit for expansion outweighed the negatives of inconsistency in process.

It is interesting to note that as Toll has become a national company and its expansion has slowed, it has become more focused on functional consistency across regions and cities, and the degree of operational latitude for project managers has declined compared to the early days.

The fact that different organizational structures gave different results was a lesson that was pretty strong in my head by the late 1990s. At the time, I had begun to focus on operational excellence; in particular, how to raise a builder's return on assets by simultaneous improvements in both cycle time (how long it takes to build a home) and quality improvement (one of the key ingredients in building a home faster).

I had experimented with the techniques needed to do this (even flow production, defect reduction initiatives, TQM, scheduling software, etc.), but the results were inconsistent. By 1996, I had finally recognized the fact that these efforts were being implemented through an organizational structure that had not changed from the early days of the company I was then running.

By changing the organizational structure to include a vice president of process control and improvement who had authority to work across the organization with the sole goal of achieving higher return on assets, I suddenly had the structural change that the MIT course had highlighted. No other builder had a similar function. By just adding another vice-president level manager who had equal standing to the operations, sales and marketing, finance and accounting, and other department heads, I had made the topic of improvement an everyday thought in everything that we did. The organization could not hide from it. Even more, the process control and improvement person had the authority to work across multiple departments in order to drive the kind of multidiscipline changes that were needed to make the organization as a whole work more productively.

Over the next several years, primarily for Arvida/ St. Joe at the Weston community in South Florida, this organizational change and function became perfected with Rich Rodriguez, a Naval Academy graduate with an MBA specializing in industrial engineering disciplines. By using his authority and position, he was able to guide us from a 16 percent return on assets to over 100 percent in about four years. The changes implemented probably numbered in the hundreds, but the key driver was to change the organizational structure and then use that structure to help implement the system changes needed to get better results.

The changes described in prior chapters concerning the improvements in warranty and permitting fell under Rich's oversight. But there were many others, also.

For example, in order to get our twenty-five home starts per week (five per day), every week and every day, we adopted a consistent set of "closed loop" meetings that involved the effort to start homes and then control their production. The meetings involved both in-house personnel (our permitting staff and senior construction managers, for example) and outside people who were critical in the house-starting function (surveyors, excavators, the plumber who did the slab plumbing, etc.). Together they would review each house "slotted" for a start over the next several weeks (usually six to eight weeks in advance).

By going through a rigorous checklist of making sure every item was in place (or scheduled to be in place) for each house for its scheduled start, a running list of "to do items" was developed and managed. The result was a smooth-flowing system that was significantly different from the prior one, where construction managers had permits dropped on their desk (like a chicken being thrown over a wall) and then told to start the house. That "old" system was characterized by chaos, and the trade subcontractors were chided and bullied in the process. It was not anyone's "best example" of an organized system. Yet, it was the way most homebuilding companies ran at the time.

The end result of the closed-loop start system was that there was an even flow of work going to the field, and that even flow then provided a relatively stable platform to begin to work on other improvements that enabled us to reduce cycle times, reduce costs, reduce defects, and improve customer and trade satisfaction. I doubt we could have done those things without having someone who had the core responsibility in the organization to change the ways we did things, mostly across functions and across our vendor base.

My summary of the organizational change lesson became: organizations tend to do the things they are organized to do.

It kind of sounded like a Yogi Berra comment, but it had the ring of truth to it and has proven true since.

Sometimes it takes a wholesale change of an organization and sometimes only a minor change to get the job done and for things to begin to happen differently. You can see the logic played out regularly in the news, both in government and in business. When the president appoints a "special envoy for Middle East peace," it is recognition that just having the State Department work on the problem is an incomplete solution. Things are looked at primarily through a diplomatic lens at State, when, in truth, diplomacy, economics, security, and a host of other considerations need to be addressed also in order to have a more comprehensive solution.

Having one senior "project manager" for the problem also focuses a singular responsibility and accountability for the effort. Leaving the solution in a functional silo also leaves open excuses for nonperformance due to inaction or uncoordinated actions from other "silos."

There is a corollary to the lesson that also applies: what organizations need to do changes with time. To think that the old organizational structure can handle the new needs is not rational. Therefore, organizations need to become adept at changing their structure and their systems if they are to continue to evolve effectively. Companies need to be willing to destroy an old organization in order to create a new one to handle new issues.

The work in breaking apart General Motors' organization in 2009 as part of its bankruptcy and rescue by the government was a recognition that the old organizational structures and managers that had grown up in that organization had to be changed if there was to be a significantly different performance in the future.

In true proof that no idea is really new, in 2009 Wally Graham, who did organizational improvement work with DMB in Phoenix, among other organizations, introduced me to a book about organizational structure. The book, *Designing Organizations for High Performance*, by David P. Hanna, was written in 1988. Espousing the same principles, Hanna notes: "All organizations are perfectly designed to get the results they get."

So, in sum, in order to get different results, oftentimes the organizational structure, as well as the systems and policies, need to be changed markedly. Companies that are organized to do this and embrace it will tend to do better than those who do not.

*"Organizations tend to do the things they are organized to do. The things that organizations must do change with time, and the organizational structure has to change, too."*

Exercise: Can you think of an organizational change that you would like to make, either in your company or in someone else's? Why? What improvement would it lead to?

_____

_____

_____

_____

_____

_____

_____

_____

_____

_____

_____

_____

_____

_____

_____

# II

## MANAGEMENT AND
## MEASUREMENTS

*The job of a manager can usually be reduced to the phrase "get it done."
There are many ways of getting things done and many tools to assist in
that endeavor. Learning what to measure and how to communicate those
measurements is an important skill to know for achieving management
success.*

If organizations are the engines that are used to achieve
business goals, measurements are the dashboard indicators that help to understand whether those goals are
being achieved and to communicate performance to
an audience.

I learned this basic lesson early in my career as a
young navy lieutenant in charge of a detachment of
Seabees (Naval Construction Battalions) in Vietnam.
The team (named Detail Bronco) had an assignment
to pioneer a road through the jungle and up a mountain to create a new radar station for the navy on the
top of that mountain.

The concept was relatively simple. Via maps and a physical excursion through the jungle, we determined the route that the road should take. Our surveyors then "rough staked" the path. Our equipment operators then would use bulldozers to clear trees and boulders and to "cut" the road into the mountainside.

Sometimes large rock formations needed to be blasted away with dynamite ("shot" in the parlance of the blasters.) A grading crew would then follow the bulldozers and more finely grade the roadway and put in any rudimentary drainage controls required to prevent major washouts in the monsoon rains that frequented Vietnam. At the end we would then stabilize the road surface with crushed gravel that we created in our own crushing plant, so that the road had some final stability.

The early going was frustrating. Progress was slow, and there was a lot of griping that the project would never be done in the time allotted. We hit more rock than we expected, and progress slowed for the blasting that needed to be done. The small bulldozers that we had were not up to the task of moving the large rocks that we found, and the equipment was breaking down frequently. Each of these problems had to be solved.

For example, to get larger bulldozers (Caterpillar D-8 models) than the smaller D-6s that were part of our detachment equipment allocation, we engineered a "trade" with the army engineers at Long Binh. Twenty cases of frozen T-bone steaks for the army equipment sergeant, which we were able to get through the navy's supply system and which the army engineers craved, facilitated one of their excess D-8s "disappearing" for several months to us.

To have gone through "channels" to requisition the bulldozer would have taken months. In the end, we were happy and they were well fed and the bulldozer was returned at the end of the job.

But equipment was only one problem. Searching for some way to try to increase our production and to let the team know about progress, I hit on the simple idea of a chart on the outside wall of the operations office.

Entitled "Bronco vs. the Mountain," it drew a rising diagonal line. The vertical axis was the number of feet of road we had pioneered, and the horizontal axis was the number of days. In a simple fashion, I showed how many lineal feet that we had to pioneer to get to the top and how many days we had to accomplish the task. If our actual performance was below the line, we were behind schedule. If we were above the line, we were ahead.

Each day, at the end of the day, the surveyors would measure the total distance of road we had pioneered to date and would come back and put a mark on the chart above that date. Quickly, it became a social event. The work crews would return at the end of the day, clean up, grab a beer, and then go over to the operations office to see the posting (it was outside on a bulletin board) of the update of the chart by the surveyors.

If we were ahead of schedule, there was much celebration, particularly if we were getting further ahead. If we were behind, discussions would develop on how to catch up. Either way, the facts were out in the open, easy to understand, and clearly communicated the goal.

In the first week or so after instituting the chart, the team performance was not much different than before. We were behind schedule and not seeming to catch up. Then, as if by magic, the line started to climb at a higher angle than the "plan line"; we were still behind, but catching up. Two weeks later, we "crossed the line" and were ahead of plan. Over the two months, the acceleration continued until the top was reached: one month ahead of schedule.

What had changed? With a clear understanding of what needed to be done and quick feedback on how the team was doing, natural competitive juices started to work. Team members started to understand how much work needed to be done each day in order to beat the schedule. The surveyors went out early each day and began to mark the point on the pioneer line that had to be made that day to beat the schedule. Then they started to mark one, two, and three days out, and the supervisors started to look for what their upcoming problems might be and to work on solutions before the problem was in their face.

In the end, though, by having a clear and concise goal and a simple, transparent measurement mechanism, the team had the tool to understand how they were doing and to help them achieve the goal we had.

I had stumbled upon the axiom: "You can't manage what you don't measure." Although attributed to Deming, the axiom really has unknown roots. Deming understood the importance of data and measuring things ("In God we trust; all others bring data") and the importance of measures in understanding whether improvements were being made. He also understood that management was about motivating and directing people toward a goal.

In that context, people can be managed without measurements, and they often are. Measurements help the manager understand trends, progress, improvements, debilitations, and where the team currently sits in a context of either a goal or past performance. Measurements in and of themselves do not manage people. They provide a tool to help provide management direction and team understanding that is dispassionate.

If key variables are measured and they, in fact, do correlate to the performance goal, those measurements can help raise the chances that management decisions will be more helpful than not in achieving a goal. However, they are not a certainty. Great managers may actually get great performance with little or no use of measurements, either through luck or great gut instincts. On the other hands, great measurement tools in the hands of a lousy manager probably do not make much of a positive difference at all.

For the cases in the middle, though, having measurements most likely leads to better performance than not, provided the measurements are truly indicative of drivers of performance. Just as organizations tend to do the things they are organized to do, but those things can change with time, measurements that were relevant for yesterday may not be relevant for tomorrow.

Once we had pioneered the road, the "Bronco vs. the Mountain" chart was no longer needed. Another measurement tied to the next task or tasks to be done had to be developed.

Organizations can become too measurement focused. It is not uncommon to see pages upon pages of measurements foisted upon a workforce or management team. The important lesson for senior managers is to limit the number of measurements to just a few that are the key drivers *at that point in time*. By allowing people to focus on the few key measures and what has to be done to achieve or improve those measures, focus is maintained and the organization's possible directions are narrowed to those most important at that point in time.

In the discussion about Rich Rodriguez's "closed-loop" start meetings at Weston in the prior chapter, the simple measurements were whether there were five starts per day and twenty-five starts per week. If that pace was maintained, we would be able to complete our job on time, four years hence, because you cannot finish a house if you do not start it.

However, it quickly became evident that just starting houses did not ensure that the houses got finished. A similar type of closed-loop meeting was needed to manage the completion and closing of homes, too, with the goal being twenty-five homes closed per week, also. Different elements had to be managed to complete a home than to start a home, but the simple measurement was always in plain sight for all to see when sitting in the Process Control room.

Whether it is house starts, house closings, or how many strikes your Little League pitcher throws compared to the total number of pitches thrown, measuring what is important at that time and for that activity is the first step to managing that activity and making improvements.

## *"You can't effectively manage what you don't measure."*

Exercise: What are the most important things that you currently have to manage? What measurements do you currently use to gauge how you are doing? Should they be different? Why?

_____

_____

_____

_____

_____

_____

_____

_____

_____

_____

_____

_____

_____

_____

_____

_____

_____

_____

_____

_____

_____

# 12

## JUICE

*Time and effort are irreplaceable assets for both individuals and organizations. If they are spent on activities that do not produce the right results at the right time or which do not produce results which are profitable in relation to their costs, the time and effort are wasted. Asking yourself, your organization, and those around you a simple question regularly will help keep this problem in perspective.*

One of a manager's most important evaluations is to decide when to continue an effort and when to change course. I have this mental image from the movie *Animal House*, when the marching band is led down a dead-end alley and just piles up against the wall at the end, but continues to try to play their song and to march onward anyway. The effort of the band continues even though the result is meaningless.

Organizations can perform the same act, also. They can set off on a path of action or have a way of doing things that has worked, and then things change. However, if the actions of the organization do not change or adapt to the new circumstances, the results can be disastrous.

In 2007, I came in as the general manager of the Verrado community in Arizona to an existing situation where leases for cell towers were being negotiated on property our company owned. The negotiations were with the giants of the industry: AT&T, Verizon, T-Mobile, Sprint, Alltel, and the like. As I got the download of the situation from the manager running the effort, he indicated that he had been working with outside architects, planners, and landscape architects on design guidelines for the towers. He had been working with attorneys and consultants on the legal language and business points for the actual tower leases. On and on it went concerning the expertise being brought to bear on the negotiation of the leases.

I then asked to have a recap of the expenses to date and the budget for all of the remaining work for the leases. To date nearly $80,000 had been spent and there was only a guess that maybe another $80,000 would be required. I then asked how much we were going to make from the leases. The answer was about $2,000 per month per lease, but the leases could be terminated upon 180 days' notice by the carrier.

I then asked the simple question: for the incremental work and expense left to go, was the juice worth the squeeze? The attorneys, architects, planners, and consultants really didn't care about the overall economics of the transaction. They were doing everything they thought should be done from a professional standpoint. However, they did not care whether the transaction was economically beneficial or not.

As it stood, it would take nearly forty months to recoup what had already been spent and another forty (maybe) for what hadn't been spent. Against a risk that the plug could be pulled after six months, there was a real question of whether any incremental expenditure, other than that required to ink the transaction, was worth the effort.

In the desire to make sure all of the bases were covered and everything was "perfect," the economics of the transaction somehow had gotten lost in the mix. The manager did not have any overt reason to overspend. He just was out of the loop with regard to the economics of the deal, and the deal was so small in relative scale that it flew under the radar of the overworked finance staff. The bottom line, though, had been a wasting of time and effort in relation to the benefit that the company would most likely receive.

In an effort to be "perfect," the economics of the deal did not make a lot of sense anymore.

I first heard the expression "Is the juice worth the squeeze" from Bob Dwyer, who handled the entitlement work for Realen Homes in Berwyn, Pennsylvania, when I worked there in the early 1990s. Bob's world was to get subdivision plans approved. Entitlements are a time- and capital-consuming effort, where costs can be loaded onto a project by a municipality during the approval process to such an extent that, even though an entitlement could be attained, the economics were so upside-down that there was no value to the entitlement. In those cases, the effort in attaining the entitlement was not worth the cost and effort of doing so. The juice was not worth the squeeze.

In one case, Bob was deep into the negotiation with a township on the exactions the town was attempting to gain in return for approval of a plan. They seemed relatively benign on first glance: changes to road widths, roadway depth specifications, offsite improvements, and the like. However, when analyzed, the costs were heavily front-loaded and could not be supported by the economics of the project itself.

The town would not budge, and the only options remaining were to accept the approval (and have a project that did not financially work), walk away from the project (and lose the money invested), or litigate (spending more money in an attempt to negotiate, through the legal system, an outcome that would be economically favorable).

The latter choice was made, but, several years later, the cost of the litigation kept piling up while the economics of the project did not improve markedly, and, ultimately, the project was abandoned. The results of continuing to spend did not justify any of the economic outcomes that were in reason. The attorneys desperately wanted to continue, but finally the economics of the transaction had to be coldly evaluated, and a decision to terminate was made.

It is against the nature of most managers to quit, and that is an understandable and good trait. However, making judgments to continue must be done in a manner that is clear-eyed and thoughtful. Economics are often a main consideration, but need not be the only one.

Many outcomes, particularly for nonprofits and charitable organizations, are less economic than humanitarian. But even in those "soft result" worlds, the efforts of managers or an organization have to be weighed against the outcome desired as opposed to other outcomes from other projects, if the same human effort was directed to that alternative, instead.

One would think that the process of assessing marginal cost and marginal benefit (economist-speak for "is the juice worth the squeeze") would be drilled into managers. However, in organizations where responsibilities are diffuse across multiple departments or divisions, sometimes those executing a task are not aware of the full financial ramifications of a decision, because they are not connected to the economics in any meaningful way.

The more I have watched businesses and even non-business undertakings, the more I have valued Bob's insight. Kenny Rogers's "know when to hold 'em and know when to fold 'em" falls into the same genre of making ongoing evaluations of when the fruits of the incremental effort are worth the costs of doing so.

As Bob so well understood, the game can change along the way, and a continuing questioning of whether the next incremental effort or cost will bear fruit worth that effort is a valuable, ticking reminder that every manager should carry in his or her head.

## *"Is the juice worth the squeeze?"*

Exercise: Are there projects or tasks where you could apply this question today? How would you work through to an evaluation? What data and what considerations would you make?

_____

_____

_____

_____

_____

_____

_____

_____

_____

_____

_____

_____

_____

_____

_____

_____

_____

_____

# 13

## RISKY BUSINESS

*Have you ever asked the question, "What business are we in, and what are the risks of that business?" If there is a lesson from the market implosions of the past several years, it is that asking this question more frequently would be a good habit to adopt. Asking whether the company's financial structure is appropriate for the level of risk of the business would be even better.*

Sometimes the most basic questions about business are not addressed. If one were to read books about management, the detailed theories of finance, marketing, production, leadership, accounting, sales, and on and on would take years, if not decades, to digest. There are checklists, graphs, and philosophies for everyone.

Yet business, at its core, is a pretty simple proposition. You provide a product or service that has value to someone else (the customer). If you can sell your product or service for more than its costs you to make it, you have a potentially profitable business. If your profits, when compared to the investment in the business, yield a reasonable return on that capital, you not only have a profitable business, but also a good investment.

Good investments tend to attract more capital over time, while bad ones do not. Businesses that are good investments and can attract capital can grow their business until such time that they are not good investments any more. It is pretty simple, really.

One question that senior managers and boards of directors need to ask continually is, "What businesses are we in, and are we correctly capitalized for those businesses?"

It seems basic, but the questions are too infrequently asked. If the questions are not asked, the risk profile of the business can change, sometimes dramatically, to the point that the business itself is put in jeopardy.

One need only look at the downfall of the insurance giant AIG to see an example. As an insurance company, AIG knew how to underwrite most risks and made great returns by correctly and conservatively underwriting insurance contracts worldwide. However, with the advent of credit default swaps, the company began to underwrite contracts that would pay off if bond debt of certain agencies or governments or companies defaulted or dropped in value. However, the underwriting assumptions on these contracts failed to understand the risks involved, and the capital needed to pay off on the policies was not adequately provided for in the company's reserves.

When the financial meltdown of 2008 occurred, AIG was caught essentially naked in having to pay off on the swaps, and only the intervention of the U.S. government prevented the company from totally foundering, and the worldwide financial system was spared a total collapse. The cost to the U.S. taxpayers was huge, and essentially the equity of one of the largest and most profitable companies in the world was wiped out.

The management and board of AIG did not understand that a piece of their business had changed and that they had not capitalized correctly for that new business and its inherent risks. (My sense is that, if the risks and the capital requirements of the credit default swap business had been truly known, AIG would not have been in the business at all.)

Some businesses are not very capital intensive. Service businesses come to mind. The core physical assets of the business might be some office space and furniture. The real assets are the employees. If the work is hand to mouth, with a book of business out one or two months, the capital at risk is oftentimes not very much. If the book of business collapses, there is a short period to understand the situation and to react. However, if the reaction time is quick enough, people could be laid off, the office equipment sold, and the business shut down. There typically is not much need for debt in these kinds of businesses and, in fact, debt would not be a great idea. With little certainty to revenues, the ability to handle debt would be difficult in a downturn.

However, if the business developed a stable book of business that became more predictable over time, the addition of some debt might be appropriate, particularly if that debt helped to either grow the business or improve the productivity and profit of the existing business.

The residential real estate business has several different facets to it. A pure "merchant" homebuilder is one who buys a lot, builds a house upon it, and then sells the house and lot to a retail homebuyer. A developer buys larger tracts of land, obtains the entitlements and permits to build upon that land, installs the site improvements on the land, and then sells finished lots to a merchant homebuilder. A builder/developer vertically integrates these two functions.

In the case of the merchant homebuilder, the risk time frame is relatively limited. It is the time it takes from the acquisition of the lot, through the time it takes to build a home on the lot, and finishes with the sale and closing of that home to a retail customer. This time period may be a year or, at the most, two years, and can actually be as low as four to six months.

Typical loans for home construction are short term, because the manufacturing process is relatively quick. Equity capital needed is relatively limited and, even though margins are relatively limited also, the returns on capital are sufficient, especially considering the relatively limited risk involved. In financial terms, the term of the assets and the liabilities are pretty evenly matched.

In the case of the developer, the game changes. It can take years to achieve entitlements, and the costs of doing so are wildly variable. There is no certainty that the entitlements envisioned will actually be granted. It can take months, if not years, to develop the site improvements on a piece of property, also.

The costs can wildly fluctuate with weather, contractor competition, commodity pricing and a host of other factors eating into potential returns. The time to finish improvements can also fluctuate considerably. Finally, the actual price for the lots at the time that they will be sold can change with the market dynamics at that time. They can be both wildly higher and wildly lower than expected. Finally, the pace at which the lots can be sold can vary considerably with the conditions of the market at points in time. Add to this the costs of carrying the land (real estate taxes, property maintenance, etc.), even before any debt service, and costs can mount up fast.

The bottom line is that development is a long-term proposition with potentially wide variations in revenues, costs, and timing. In a good market, a lot of money can be made, and in a bad market, the entire investment can be lost. The ability to hold until the market is better is critical to just having a chance to get your capital back when times turn bad.

In development, the addition of debt is treacherous. Unless there are other sources of cash flow to support the debt when lots are not being sold, debt is risky. Because the development asset is usually long-term asset, if debt is taken, it usually should be longer-term debt, rather than short term. Because of these risks, development is usually best capitalized with patient equity in sufficient quantity to be able to ride a market cycle and be harvested in good markets (not dumped by force at deep discounts when markets are stressed).

This past economic cycle saw many homebuilders choose to expand from being merchant builders to being builder/developers for a variety of reasons. Builders were worried about not being able to attain building lots from developers in a hot market. With no lots, they faced the prospect of, perhaps, having to go out of business. So many builders became developers, too, in order to ensure their supply of lots and, by extension, their ability to survive.

With relationships with banks that had provided their construction financing, the bankers continued to provide funding to the builders on terms that more closely aligned to the models that the builders enjoyed as merchant builders: high leverage and short terms.

This was done without full recognition that the builder's business had changed to include the risks of development. When the market did decline and revenues dried up, the builders and their bankers found themselves with short-term liabilities coming due, no cash flow to service the debt, and an illiquid, long-term asset (land and building lots).

This toxic combination meant that builders lost most of their equity, banks foreclosed on illiquid assets and had to take further write-downs, and asset values in general became impaired.

The core lesson that had been ignored was that the business that builders were in had changed, but the way they had capitalized for the business had not. The results were catastrophic, with many building companies and banks being forced out of business and thousands of jobs wiped out.

Whether it is as an owner/operator, investment manager, banker, or investor, remembering to ask the most basic question regularly will help you to steer from trouble.

## *"Understand what business you are in and capitalize appropriately for the risks of that business."*

Exercise: What are the risks of your business? Do you think that you are capitalized correctly for them? Why? What would you change?

_____

_____

_____

_____

_____

_____

_____

_____

_____

_____

_____

_____

_____

_____

_____

_____

_____

_____

_____

# 14

## GOING IN HOCK

*A decision to be either a borrower or a lender carries burdens that need to be carefully evaluated. The events of the Great Recession have reminded many of these burdens and some quick thoughts to remember about debt financing. One of them is that before you can achieve a return on capital, you must first have a return of capital.*

*Neither a borrower nor a lender be; for*
*loan doth oft lose both itself*
*and friend, and borrowing dulls the edge of husbandry.*

**William Shakespeare**
*Hamlet*

In thinking about how businesses and individuals capitalize themselves, particularly over the past quarter-century, readily available and relatively low cost debt grew into the preferred vehicle of choice.

Ready availability, enabled in part by the ability to securitize and to hedge downside risk, masked the risks of debt to both the lender and to the borrower.

In some ways, the stigma of debt and the inability to pay off debt had been lost over a generation. Although debtors' prisons were a thing of the past, even up through the 1960s there was a stigma of not being able to pay off one's debts. The social out-casting from society (or the possibility of it) served to keep people in check with regard to their incurrence of debt.

Local banks, the normal lenders to small business and to individuals, were part of a community, and the social pressures and trust nature of banks (the money they lent was often that of the community's citizens, so there was a veneer of social responsibility in every lending decision) served as a governor on excessive lending and borrowing.

However, with a more mobile society starting in the 1960s, the advent of portable credit from faceless organizations (credit cards and loans from big national and international banks), and a loosening of the bankruptcy codes for businesses and individuals, the social contract that served as the governor on excessive lending began to deteriorate. If you didn't pay your debts, it went unnoticed in communities that were ever more transient. The social stigma to taking on debt was declining.

The advent of securitization of debt, whether it was credit card debt pools or mortgage pools or pools of car or consumer loans, moved the interface between borrower and lender even further apart. The lender and borrower, instead of meeting on the street or in the local coffee shop, now did not know who the other party was.

An investment fund in Iceland along with a mutual fund in the United States and a teacher's retirement fund in Oregon could all own a piece of an Albany, New York couple's consumer loan on the refrigerator they bought from Sears. If the couple did not pay, a debt collection company from Nashville might try to collect the debt, but the owners of the debt and the couple would never have to face each other directly. The result is the further deterioration of the stigmas of debt from both the borrower and lender side of the table.

If there has been a lesson from the Great Recession, it is that debt has a downside for multiple parties. As we have seen on the housing side, the relatively easy access to debt to buy houses and other assets (via home equity loans) stretched borrowers and, when the economy declined, many have had to give up their homes and assets (not to mention their credit rating).

Similarly, on the corporate side, extensive borrowing (particularly in the overnight repo market) has brought down some of the icons of finance (Lehman Brothers and Bear Stearns), as they were unable to roll their short-term debt over in a declining market. On the lender side, the scores are still being tallied in terms of the number of banks going out of business. The cost to taxpayers for government bailouts of lenders and banks will probably top a trillion dollars.

In 2009, I had the opportunity to mentor a dozen "Young Leaders" of the Urban Land Institute in Phoenix. Typically aged between twenty-eight and thirty-five, this was their first experience with recession as adults. In our first meeting, I asked them each to bring in ten lessons they had learned so far in the downturn. Interestingly, nearly all came in with an observation that debt was not a good thing, either for them or for the company they worked for. It sounded like a conversation with my parents and grandparents who had lived through the Depression.

I noted to them that the first risk of debt is that it is only as good as the underwriting of risk of the borrower and the security. The second risk is that, when the underwriting is faulty, the borrower's equity can be wiped out and the lender may not be able to recoup their principal, much less their principal plus a return.

One of the first precepts of finance is that before you can get a return *on* capital, you must first get a return *of* capital.

I was encouraged that the group of Young Leaders had taken what they had seen and experienced, internalized it, evaluated it, and had come up with a lesson that they both remembered and were starting to act upon.

If there is a simple lesson to be learned from the events of the Great Recession, it is that even if you can borrow, it doesn't mean that you should. And even if you can lend, it doesn't mean that you should, either. There are many borrowers who saw their equity wiped out by borrowing, because the loan rate looked so much better than the cost of equity, and many lenders who saw their equity wiped out, because they incorrectly underwrote the risks of the loan they were making.

It is a hard lesson to learn, but a good one to remember for all concerned.

*"Just because you **can** borrow doesn't mean that you should; and just because you **can** lend, doesn't mean that you should, either."*

Exercise: Can you think of an instance, either personally or businesswise, where this lesson would apply? What was it? What led you to your conclusion?

_____

_____

_____

_____

_____

_____

_____

_____

_____

_____

_____

_____

_____

_____

_____

_____

_____

_____

_____

_____

# 15

## GROWTH BY ACQUISITION

*Growth of a company's business provides opportunity for employees and investors to profit. However, growth by acquisition, particularly a large acquisition, offers a particular set of risks that have to be considered very carefully.*

Thinking about the businesses in which a company chooses to compete and how the company capitalizes itself for those businesses, an interesting corollary applies in the area of acquisitions and the risks attendant to those acquisitions.

Businesses can choose to grow "organically" (that is, by growing their business year after year through the incremental expansion of customers, markets, products, and the like) or through acquisitions that allow them to "leapfrog" to a greater size or a different market footprint overnight.

Either strategy has its own risks and rewards. Either strategy also requires a different capital structure to minimize the risk of the strategy.

Each of the major economic booms that the United States has had over the past five decades has been marked by stories of overexpansion and the come-uppance that inevitably results. Whether it was the expansions of Tyco or Citibank into multiple lines of business, or the "synergistic" acquisition of America Online by Time Warner, or the acquisition of Countrywide Mortgage by Bank of America, each of these supposedly strategic business moves ended or appears to be ending in a very bad result for the executives who drove the acquisition, the shareholders of the acquirer, the employees of the acquired company, the financial firms who financed the acquisition, or some combination of all of these parties.

Not all acquisitions end in disaster, but there are enough stories of acquisitions gone bad to make at least a basic case for hesitation when the opportunity to acquire presents itself.

Organic growth also has issues. An expansion strategy that is wrong takes a long time to develop and, by the time that the strategy's outcomes are known, there may be little time to adjust, if the strategy was truly a bad one. However, because of the relatively slow-moving nature of organic expansion, there are multiple opportunities to evaluate the strategy and the current outcomes against expectations and to adjust midstream.

One can think of Walmart's expansion, both geographically and product wise, over the past several decades as a good example. By expanding within the United States and then overseas with a basic model, each step provided a way to learn while growing. The addition of groceries, pharmacies, gas stations, and other services to the basic store allowed each location to expand revenue opportunities with very little incremental cost.

Walmart is probably not a merger-and-acquisition banker's friend, because it seems to shun the idea of leapfrog expansion via acquisition. It also is not making huge, one-time bets that could either be drastically right or drastically wrong. In addition, the cultural issues of acquisition are minimized via internal growth. Absorbing people who have grown in a different culture can sap productivity and benefits that might theoretically accrue by an acquisition.

Acquisitions have risks that are unique. One of these risks is the risk of illiquidity of the asset acquired. One rule that seems to apply is: the larger the size of the acquisition, the fewer the number of potential bidders for the asset. With the smallness of potential bidders comes the risk that the asset could become illiquid if the acquirer wants to resell. Value is established both at a point in time and based on a particular need or strategy. If those change with time, value can change, also, both for the better and for the worse.

A good example is the Japanese acquisition binge on American real estate assets in the late 1980s and early 1990s, including trophy real estate assets such as the Pebble Beach Golf Course and Rockefeller Center. Financed by available and inexpensive debt from the Japanese banks and industry, the assets were purchased at a significant premium (reflecting their "trophy" status and the resultant benefit to the egos of the acquirer).

As often happens, several years later the premium was unjustified, the debts came due, and there were no new acquirers in the wings for other than bargain-basement pricing. Losses were felt by both the acquirer and its lenders and investors, and the repercussions are still being felt in Japan today.

Whether it is real estate assets that are in play or companies being acquired, the risks of illiquidity and thin market valuations have to be taken seriously.

In the real estate boom of the 1970s and 1980s, Houston benefitted from an oil-fueled boom in employment, and one of the beneficiaries was U.S. Home, a regional homebuilder that expanded onto the national stage quickly. As one of the few public homebuilders, U.S. Home had ready access to capital and used that capital to acquire large parcels of land as part of its expansion.

In the inevitable downturn, it found itself highly leveraged and very long on land and had to seek bankruptcy protection to restructure its business and financing, which was done under the guidance of Isaac Heimbinder, an attorney brought in to oversee U.S. Homes' rebirth. In looking at the asset- and debt-laden company, Isaac stated that obvious fact that is the warning to all on an acquisition binge: "You can buy more land in an afternoon than you can get rid of in a lifetime."

Whether it is lots, buildings, golf courses, companies, or financial assets, such as slices of collateralized loans that suddenly go out of favor, the illiquidity risk of large and bulk acquisitions have to be considered carefully by wise managers who understand that often the best deal is the one not inked.

## *"You can buy more land in an afternoon than you can get rid of in a lifetime."*

Exercise: Are there any observations that you have regarding growth? What are they, and how did you learn them?

_____

_____

_____

_____

_____

_____

_____

_____

_____

_____

_____

_____

_____

_____

_____

_____

_____

_____

_____

_____

# 16

## NUMBER KNOWLEDGE

*In flush times, management attention is often best spent growing the business' top line. However, when times turn tough, knowing your overall financial and operating situation becomes critical to the existence of the business. The tool for this knowledge is the "numbers"; the key indicators for the business.*

No matter what business you are in, inevitably you have to endure a downturn. If acquisitions (particularly those done at a premium to book value) are an indicator of an upturn, retrenchments and divestitures are an indicator of a downturn. Growth and good times are a narcotic for business that lead to some decisions that, in retrospect, are head scratchers. As much as one can caution against those decisions, they inevitably happen, even to the best of companies. You cannot repeal human nature.

It is how companies and their managers respond to downturns that is the true measure of their worth. When the economic winds are in your face, rather than at your back, the impact of both good and bad decisions, effective management teams, and competent execution capability can be assessed.

The real estate industry is notorious for its cycles, most often driven by great gobs of capital coming into the asset class and overinflating fundamental values. Sooner or later that over inflation is corrected by a downturn that causes asset values to collapse below their fundamental value. Those who acquired at the top lose value and those who acquire near the bottom attain value. In the process, there are lessons that seem to apply over and over on how to handle a downturn that, once learned, can help to mitigate the effects of the downturn and can leave a company in a position to profit in the upturn.

The first lesson is an outgrowth of "In God we trust; all others bring data." In this case the simple lesson is: "Know your numbers."

Captured in the simple three words are a lot of important concepts, however. The first is that knowing your numbers also means trusting your numbers. A manager needs to know that the data he or she is reviewing is true. There has to have been enough trial on the data to know that it is truly representative of what is being measured. The second is that the numbers are measuring things that truly are important to the business's core health at that point in time.

For example, sales numbers are a key piece of data for most enterprises. Unit sales, dollar volume of sales, cancellation rates, what categories of customers are buying, what is the trend of those purchases, what sales people are making sales, who is not selling, what is their conversion rate, and on and on. In good times, sales numbers might be reviewed weekly or even monthly. In tough times, they may have to be reviewed daily or even hourly. Remember: Shy salespeople have skinny kids.

In early 2008, as the recent real estate downturn was really beginning to be felt in the Phoenix market, this lesson came home to bear for me. As the master planned community developer at Verrado, we ran a sales and information center for the community and for the benefit of the builders (to whom we had sold lots) who were selling homes in the community. Even though we had been paid a substantial base amount for the lots we had sold to the builders, we received additional contingent payments (based on the actual sale price of homes) at the time of the closing of escrow for each home with retail homebuyers. We additionally received other fees (impact fees, utility reimbursements, and marketing reimbursements) that were tied to the sale of homes.

These contingent payments and fees amounted to significant amounts of money and were one of our core sources of revenue. Knowing what our builders were doing on the sales front was important for us to understand our upcoming revenue streams. In the earlier good times, exact tracking of revenue streams was loose. It would not be uncommon to have several hundred thousand dollars just "appear" because we were not aware that sales had occurred and, when they did and the escrow agent collected our sums due and paid us, it was a "pleasant surprise."

Pleasant surprises might be nice for Christmas or a birthday, but it is not a recommended strategy for running a business.

As the market became more difficult and cash became tighter, we had to fully review and adjust our data collection system. Weekly calls to both sales agents for the builders and the title companies were used to try to get certainty on sales and cancellations, dollar value of sales in escrow, when houses would close, and when we would be getting our distribution from the closing.

When a "surprise" did occur, we studied how it had slipped through the system and tried to figure out corrective mechanisms for the future. Instead of scrubbing our data once a quarter, we did it monthly. In this way we could track where there seemed to be defects or holes in our information and then figure out a way to get more accurate information.

Along the way, we used the data more creatively to figure out which community-focused advertising support programs were working (was the juice worth the squeeze) and which could be dropped. We became very creative at finding out what our competitors were doing on a highly frequent basis to see if our builders' performance was just part of a general market trend or was better (or worse) than the competition. If it was significantly better or worse, we tried to figure out why, so we could pass on the insights to them. When it became apparent that there was an overall market slide happening, we significantly pulled back on advertising (don't put the hay down until the goats are eating) and shifted our support to other efforts that seemed to be having a more direct effect. We experimented a lot, but we were comfortable that the data we were collecting and acting upon was good.

A similar effort occurred on the cost side. The money spent to put in roads, sewers, water lines, and such was the largest cost center. This development spending was typically reviewed once a quarter and carried a lot of cushion in the budgets. It was not uncommon to overestimate the development spending by several million dollars per month.

In flush times, such "conservative" projections were welcomed. However, as the slowdown became more evident, more exacting cash-needs forecasting was required. To do this, weekly sessions (rather than the previous quarterly sessions) between the controllers and the development project managers started to flush out what was reality and what was cushion. In the process, which took nearly six months to get working well, much more reliable cash needs were developed. Even more important, the heightened regular scrutiny enabled more creative solutions for finding revenue or reducing expenses to be executed more frequently.

The point is that, in both cases, the frequency and certainty of data had to become much more exacting as the downturn progressed in order to allow for appropriate actions to be taken quickly. One can argue that these systems should have been done in the good times, anyway, and that would be true. However, even more true, is that in a downturn the data needed is oftentimes subtly different from that required in a strong market.

To know, when the downturn does hit, that stepping up the frequency of the kinds of data needed for whatever are the most important functions at that time, is really the lesson to remember.

## *"Know your numbers."*

Exercise: What numbers do you know so well that you carry them around in your head? Why are they that important? Are there numbers you think that you should know better?

_____

_____

_____

_____

_____

_____

_____

_____

_____

_____

_____

_____

_____

_____

_____

_____

_____

_____

_____

_____

_____

_____

# 17

## WALKING TO FIND REALITY

*Knowing critical facts through numbers is important for a manager. Knowing and feeling reality by walking around is equally important, particularly in tough times. Once reality is understood, acting fast to make changes then becomes paramount.*

Numbers are only numbers until they are put into a context. One is a number. One foot converts the abstract "one" into a measure of distance. But one foot becomes relevant only in the context of how it compares to other distances. One foot is less than one mile by a lot and greater than one inch by twelve times. One foot to a golf course developer isn't very much, but one foot to a surveyor laying out a foundation close to a property line is a lot.

In business, numbers give measurement and relativity to a variety of items: sales volume, cash flow, cash balances, amounts owed, number of defects, and so forth. Each of these is important in its own context to help understand relative size, progress, or some other measure of organizational performance.

In a downturn, the numbers that we use to measure business performance are critical to understanding the reality that is actually confronting the enterprise. The larger the enterprise, the more this is so. In a small business, an owner/operator is most often close to the action and can sense on a very real-time basis what is going on with the business. If no one is showing up at the shop and or the phone is not ringing, it is very evident by the sounds and rhythms of the operations that something is amiss.

In larger companies, the ability to know the reality of what is going on becomes harder. Managers cannot be physically present at the locations of business operations all of the time.

Numbers help to see reality, but physical presence is even more critical. Management by walking around is an important skill for senior managers to acquire. Visiting operations regularly, shopping competition personally, and talking to front-line employees about what they are seeing are among the methods that a manager should employ to try to come to a point of view regarding the reality that faces the business.

In military lore, the best commanders want to be near the front so that they know the reality of the situation sooner than not, so that they can determine the best orders to give to exploit the situation to their advantage.

In business, the ability to ascertain the reality of a given moment sooner than one's competition gives advantage. In upturns, that advantage might mean that an opportunity to prosper is not lost. In downturns, it might be the difference between survival and extinction.

The combination of good numbers and first-hand management knowledge of the on-the-ground situation is nearly unbeatable in a downturn. Unfortunately, in a downturn, management tends to pull itself into a cocoon of isolation in its efforts to manage during the crisis. This detachment from the reality of the external world actually serves a detrimental purpose. The only reality is that of reported numbers and the filtered input from others. First-hand exposure to the environment becomes lost in the decision-making process.

In late 2006, as the real estate downturn really began to take hold nationally, Christopherson Homes, Inc. had homebuilding operations in Sonoma County, California, and in the Sacramento area. As the market worsened, we began to do more frequent (quarterly) and disciplined analyses of our competitors in an effort to have first-hand knowledge of what was selling and what was not and why. These analyses helped to give a good background to the marketplace and our response to it. Our competitors often waited to receive quarterly reports from consultants who attempted to provide some of this background, but the data was four to five months old by the time it was received and digested.

Ours, gathered by our own managers and sales personnel, was up to date and fresher.

Even more important, we had reorganized into a project manager system, taking what had been functional managers and making them responsible for individual projects. Although not necessarily fully trained as project managers, the idea was to have a singular focus of knowledge and accountability for each project. Having the responsibility for the project as a whole and then having a singular point of accountability for execution of strategies was more important at that time than the efficiencies gained by having functional managers.

On a frequent (biweekly) basis, the top management of the company would go on-site with the project manager to review issues at their project and to personally visit selected competitors who seemed to be doing well. This method of visitation and quick, on-the-spot decisions of what to do to be more competitive allowed our communities to adapt more quickly to the changing marketplace.

For example, it became evident in the early visits that job-site cleanliness was not up to par. In the heady days of the boom market, the discipline of keeping a clean construction site had been lost. By focusing on a clean job site, our communities began to look perceptibly better than those of our competitors. Understanding that first impressions can help shape buying decisions, we wanted to make sure that our first impression for both our existing residents and our prospects was always the best.

Raw numbers could not convey what was obvious to the eye.

Needless to say, by focusing on job site cleanliness, we did not win the affection of some of our superintendents or trade partners. In fact, some quit because they felt that they were being held to a standard not common in the marketplace. However, we felt that cleanliness was an important differentiator and held the course.

We also saw in the on-site visits that the homes that had mature-looking landscaping really stood out in a positive way. In the practice of the industry at the time, builders only provided a minimal amount of base landscaping with the home. The customer was left to install more elaborate landscaping in the next year (or two or three) after they moved in. The result was an uneven and sometimes unfinished look to the streetscape of the community.

For the homes that did have finished landscaping, though, we noticed that having large olive trees in the front yard tended to not only make the home look stately, but made the street look more exclusive and finished. We wondered whether we could make every home we delivered look that good. If we did, we would have a community that would look and feel more expensive and completed than our competition.

At the time, discounts from list price (an unheard-of phenomenon in the prior several years) were becoming necessary to sell homes in a market that was really beginning to deteriorate. As an experiment, we began to extensively landscape our unsold "spec" homes and included the mature trees as part of the program. Costing nearly $25,000 per home, it was an amount that was actually less than the discounts being offered at the time by our competitors. The experiment showed that, as soon as the landscaping was completed, the home would sell.

Taking a hint from this, we began to include a more extensive landscape package on every home. This resulted in a more completed-looking streetscape for the whole community and a significant differentiator from the neighborhoods of our competitors. Our sales rates got better.

As the market continued to decline, we were able to sell houses, albeit at less profit than we had before, but still at paces higher than any of our competitors. We finished our building operations and sold out of the community before the market really got bad. Many of our competitors never made it to the finish line. They were either foreclosed upon by their lender or went bankrupt.

By dealing with the reality of the marketplace on a real-time basis, by knowing what our competitive environment was by having good data, and by having management be on site and walking around to assess the asset and make quick decisions to adapt to the marketplace, we were able to navigate the downturn better than most.

The lesson is an enduring one. It is critical to find reality and deal with it...fast! This skill is even more critical when things are unwinding and the market is in distress. Only through the use of good data and seasoned eyes can reality be understood and a plan to adapt to reality formulated.

But, speed is just as important. Reality can change and, with it, the appropriateness of response can also.

# *"Walk around, find reality, and deal with it…fast!"*

Exercise: What are the best methods you have seen for finding out business reality? Have you seen "managing by walking around" succeed? Fail? Why?

_____

_____

_____

_____

_____

_____

_____

_____

_____

_____

_____

_____

_____

_____

_____

_____

_____

_____

_____

_____

_____

# 18

## INERTIA

*Psychology is an important factor in a customer's buying decision. The fact that a company is active and moving forward, especially in slow markets, will enable sales to happen. The inertia of a company is just as important as the economics of the product.*

Psychology is a critical element in business success and failure. How customers feel determines, in part, what they do.

We are used to seeing this in the business cycle the longer we live. In good times, we see the glass as half full and tend to take risks under the assumption that things will remain good or that things will work out. We have a positive mind-set. In bad times, we pull in our horns and the darkest thoughts prevail. We worry that we will lose our home, our job, our company, our money, or other things of value. We tend to then get very conservative with our decisions, and that very conservatism tends to make the bad times self-fulfilling. The glass is now half empty.

However, even in a downturn, businesses can survive and sometimes prosper. This differentiation has to do, in part, with the psychology of the business, its employees, and its customers. Those who choose to find and accept the reality of the situation and then act quickly have a leg up on those who do not. But finding and dealing with reality can miss the important component of psychology for both the business and the customer.

When an organization has a purpose and is doing something, it has a different psyche and puts off a different feeling to those who come in contact with people in the organization. This becomes even more critical when times are bad and the prevailing wisdom is negative.

I learned the lesson early in my career in the real estate downturn of the early 1980s. With mortgage rates in the mid- to high teens, the housing market faced tough headwinds. With soaring unemployment across most sectors of the economy, consumer confidence was low, too. Yet, people still needed houses. The baby boom was just coming into its prime home-buying years and families were growing. The base need for more housing was there, even if the confidence to act was not.

At Toll Brothers, we were building homes in Philadelphia's northern suburbs and in the towns around Princeton, New Jersey, at the time. We had the benefit of having two major markets that supported jobs (New York and Philadelphia) and a diverse banking sector that included many savings and loan banks (S&Ls).

As the economy got worse and mortgage rates rose, the pool of buyers was reduced, but not eliminated.

The reality was that you had to learn to capture the smaller pool and still make money.

The first step in the process was learning how to financially engineer our mortgage loan offerings so that buyers could afford to buy our homes. Working with local mortgage brokers and banks, we learned to do 3-2-1 buydowns on thirty-year fixed-rate mortgages in order to help people qualify. An 11 percent loan would have an 8 percent interest rate for the first year, 9 percent for the second, 10 percent for the third, and 11 percent thereafter, with the hope that, by the time the loan got to the full rate, the market would stabilize and rates would be lower, permitting a refinance (and it did). People would qualify in those days at the 8 percent rate, rather than the 11 percent rate. That has now changed,

We learned how to do straight buydowns by paying points up front in return for a lower permanent rate. We learned about a new kind of mortgage called an ARM (adjustable rate mortgage). We learned to buy forward commitments for mortgages. All of this learning was based on the understanding that, even if people loved our homes and communities and thought that the pricing was fair, if they could not get a mortgage that worked with their income, no sale could be transacted.

We experimented with programs, offering them in ads in the local newspapers. We did outreach programs to Realtors to announce our mortgage affordability initiatives. Our sales force made calls to old prospects to let them know what was new.

In our communities, we made a decision to keep a limited amount of "spec" homes in production, so that inventory was available quickly. At the same time, having "sticks going in the air" gave a feeling of activity in the community. We managed the process closely, always making sure that carpenters were visible. We encouraged our subcontractors to work weekends, when most of our customers came out to shop, and to take time off during the week when customers were not there. We chose our spec home locations so that the building was readily visible to customers coming into the community.

Essentially, we learned that we were managing a "show" for potential customers to demonstrate that building was still occurring in the community, despite the hard times.

The combination of having inventory, having mortgage programs, and having activity was different than most of our competitors. We were showing life while others were moribund, waiting for a return to "normal."

The activity on the project convinced some customers that we were a safer bet than our competitors, who looked and felt "dead." In a decision involving one of the largest investments a family can make, relative certainty that the right decision is being made is highly important. The herd instinct comes to play, also. If others are buying and making their decision, it confirms my decision.

Activity begets activity.

Since then, the axiom has proven itself over and over again. Even in the most recent economic downturn, those builders who kept a lively sales office and showed activity in the field tended to garner more sales than those who went very conservative, limited the hours of their sales offices, and would only build on contract, which meant they did not build much at all.

Even though the open and active strategy was risky, it tended to produce less dire economic results than a strategy of battening down the hatches. Even in the direst times, a product or service can be sold and showing activity to your customer base is a good way to stay in business.

## *"Activity begets activity."*

Exercise: Are there any rules of thumb that you apply when business begins to slow down in order to stay competitive? Why?

_____

_____

_____

_____

_____

_____

_____

_____

_____

_____

_____

_____

_____

_____

_____

_____

_____

_____

_____

_____

# 19

## AN ACTION IMPERATIVE

*Managers set the tempo for how an organization behaves, both in good times and in bad. Particularly in bad times, acting quickly, even with imperfect information, can be the difference between survival and extinction.*

The great eighteenth-century British essayist Dr. Samuel Johnson wrote: *"Depend upon it, sir, when a man knows he is to be hanged in a fortnight, it concentrates his mind wonderfully"* (from *Boswell's Life of Johnson*). In modern linguistics, this is oftentimes restated as: "Nothing focuses the mind more than a pending execution."

The essence, though, is the same. When faced with extinction, the mind and spirit tend to focus on the effort not to become extinct (at least not yet). Creativity and an imperative toward action become the order of the day. Wasted time cannot be endured.

Economic downturns offer the possibility of death or extinction for a business, yet the responses to that possibility become widely varied among enterprises. Part of this can be attributed to the fact that, in some enterprises, senior managers and their employees just do not understand how dire the circumstances are or might be. They take no action to reduce the possibility of extinction.

Not knowing one's numbers or not understanding the reality of the situation can be prime culprits. However, even companies that do understand the reality of the situation can still fail if there is no true imperative to act and act quickly. Larger organizations with entrenched bureaucracies are often poster children for this problem.

In good times, not acting quickly can result in an opportunity lost or not fully capitalized upon. In bad times, it can be fatal.

One need only look at the U.S. automakers to understand the situation. For nearly two decades, General Motors had issues with quality, declining market share, a bloated cost structure, and a generally failing business model. Despite widespread knowledge of the severity of the circumstance, no concerted action was taken to truly remedy the root causes of the situation until the entire economy went into freefall in 2008. A government financial intervention and subsequent bankruptcy proceeding began to force meaningful change to address the reality of the marketplace and the deficiencies of the company's strategy and structure.

A near wholesale cleaning of management and the board was needed in order to get the organization to act differently and with a high degree of urgency.

Although caught in a similar circumstance in terms of industry and the economy, Ford seemed to be more proactive in undertaking changes. It changed its strategy, structure, and management before the severe economic downturn of 2008 and managed to survive without direct government aid and a bankruptcy. The will and speed to deal with new strategies to address the new realities that faced the business was the key differentiator.

This bias toward action has its downside. Sometimes acting quickly involves acting with incomplete information, which, in turn, can result in an action that is incorrect or off target, had the full information been known. However, knowing the relative "severity" of the general business environment can help guide actions here, with severe situations forcing faster evaluations and decisions.

In early 2006, Christopherson Homes, in northern California, was building homes and developing communities in Sacramento and Sonoma County. I had arrived as the new chief executive officer from the East Coast, where I had watched the beginning of the housing downturn and saw the impacts. My board positions on building companies in Michigan and Colorado also led me to believe that the severity of the impending downturn was going to be high and it was going to be a national phenomenon.

At the time, northern California was still in the bubble, and the market, although slowing down, was not as dire as some of the other national markets. Builders in northern California had known good times for more than a decade, and home prices had nearly doubled over the past three to five years. Land was seemingly always in short supply, so being long on land had been a prudent and necessary strategy to make money and to remain in business.

Since land entitlements in California are long (two to ten years), even if a piece of land is optioned, the costs for entitlements, planning, and architecture can run in the millions-of-dollars-per-year range over multiple years. The company had significant land holdings and future entitlement work under way, and the monthly costs were substantial.

Reviewing the situation with our board of directors, it seemed prudent to cut back on the spending we were doing to attain entitlements and to defer, wherever possible, the purchase of new tracts of land until we were certain that the market was not in true freefall.

Although a controversial call, it ended up being the correct one. As the market worsened, many of our competitors continued to buy land and spend on entitlements, even though their revenues from their homebuilding operations began to decline significantly. By looking weekly at the sales trends for both our communities and the market in general, we began to take a viewpoint that, until we could see a sustained improvement trend, we were going to assume that things would continue to get worse and act accordingly.

Looking at the historic ratios of median home price to median income, particularly in Sacramento, the ratio had climbed from a norm of about 4:1 in the 1980s and 1990s to nearly 9:1 in 2007. If one assumed that the ratio *might* return to its long-term average, it implied that home prices *might* drop to half of the then current pricing (which they ultimately did).

Even if they did not drop by that much, it seemed reasonable to assume that they would drop somewhat. If this assumption was true, then any inventory that we had built, but not closed, would devalue quickly, and we would be facing the possibility of a continual declining market.

In this situation, the strategy would be to either renegotiate or get out of any pending land deals and to cut entitlement outlays to preserve cash. Additionally we should sell any completed inventory homes at whatever price the market would bear, because it would be worth less tomorrow than it was worth today. We also should try to move through our remaining lots (again at whatever the market would bear) with either existing product that was priced lower or, where possible, with newer, smaller, simpler product that was priced lower.

All of this was contrary to the prevailing wisdom that had ruled in the prior decade (land is dear; things are worth more tomorrow than they are worth today; after all, this *is* California).

As it turned out, the strategy partially worked. We did work our way through several of the communities and got out ahead of the avalanche, but some of the larger land and lot holdings had just too much of a trail of unbuilt-upon lots to make up. In most cases, though, we did better overall than most of our competitors by acting quickly and based upon the data we were seeing, rather than past performance or wishful thinking.

In Michael Lewis's book *The Big Short,* he describes how the subprime mortgage crisis blew up into the Great Recession through the eyes of hedge fund traders who took the unconventional bet that the housing market and the financial industry would deteriorate severely in 2007. What is striking in the book is how many smart people held to the old wisdom that housing prices would always rise and bond ratings from Moody's and Standard & Poor's were always right, despite growing data to the contrary. Those who acted quickly to the new reality at least saved some of their position and capital. Those who did not got wiped out.

It is a great lesson to remember: acting fast is almost always better than acting slow.

*"No action, no traction.*
*Have a bias toward action."*

Exercise: Can you describe a situation where quick business action made a positive difference? How about a negative difference? What did you learn?

_____

_____

_____

_____

_____

_____

_____

_____

_____

_____

_____

_____

_____

_____

_____

_____

_____

# 20

## CASH

*Cash is oxygen for a business enterprise. Lacking cash can kill a business quickly, so knowing cash and projecting cash flows are critical to the survival of the enterprise, particularly in slow times.*

When times are good and business is flush, managers and entire organizations tend to take cash availability for granted. Free cash flow from operations can easily be augmented by line lending from willing banks or debt issuances, either through private or public markets. Managers tend to play offense in their thinking and look for sales growth, market share expansion, geographic expansion, product line diversification, and other investments.

Cash flows to new ideas because they seem to hold the key to even more opportunity and more profitability in the future. Saving for a rainy day goes to the back burner.

The measurement of how a company is doing financially usually comes in the form of financial statements, usually issued monthly or quarterly. Couched in the jargon of GAAP (Generally Accepted Accounting Principles), financial statements portray how the company is doing.

However, the more one deals with GAAP financial statements, the more one realizes that what the statements can portray can be vastly out of sync with the realities of the day-to-day operations of the business from a cash standpoint.

For example, I could make a widget for $1 and sell it tomorrow for $3 and show a $2 "profit" on my financial statement. A competitor could be in the same business and do the same transaction, but instead, it could spend $10 on a machine that might help it be more efficient in distributing or making its widget.

Assume that the machine had an expected life of ten years; the company would depreciate the machine at about $1 per year or about 8 cents per month, so its financial statement for the month would be revenues of $3, costs of $1, and depreciation of 8 cents, for a profit of $1.92 for the month.

However, from a cash standpoint, its revenues were $3, its production costs $1, and its outlay for the machine was $10, meaning that its cash was actually *negative* $8 for the month.

The cash might have come from money in the cash box or borrowing from the bank or an additional equity investment into the company by its owners. Either way, the second company generated less cash for the month than the first company. Granted, it had a machine that was supposedly worth $10 at the end of the month, where the first company had no such machine. But if one were to look at the income statement of the two companies, the second would look only slightly less profitable than the first for the month, yet its cash needs were significantly higher. It needed $11 (a $10 machine plus $1 to buy the widget to sell) while the first company only needed $1 to buy the widget. That is an eleven fold increase in cash need.

With multiple sources of income statement adjustments flowing each month (marking assets to market, depreciation and amortization estimates, estimates of bad receivables, etc.), GAAP income statements are a poor short-term measuring stick of a business's financial health in the thing that really matters: the oxygen of cash.

Cash is the true oxygen that enterprises run upon. If cash becomes a scarce commodity and is running out, the actions that a company must take become ever more focused on short-term needs instead of long-term opportunity, and the change can happen overnight (a severe case of "nothing focusing the mind like a pending execution"). If the company has taken cash for granted and does not have in place sophisticated tools to project cash and manage cash tightly, the precipice can be reached all too quickly, with potentially catastrophic results.

I was on the board of a builder/developer that had, so the board thought, relatively sophisticated financial controls. We had well-analyzed GAAP financial statements each month. Things looked pretty good.

In the real estate business, it is not uncommon to have to invest significant sums of money in getting new projects approved through the city and to have engineering and architectural plans completed long before the property was actually acquired and physical work started. Several million dollars of such investment per project is not unusual. From a financial statement standpoint, these expenses are "capitalized." They are treated as an asset and do not run through the income statement until the land is put into production and homes are sold, oftentimes several years in the future.

When the market started to head south in 2006 and 2007, the management team at the company recommended that a certain project be abandoned, as its economic feasibility had been diminished by the declining market to the point that it was not a good investment anymore (is the juice worth the squeeze?).

However, when the capitalized costs of the project were added up, they were well over $1 million, which took the board by surprise. We did not realize that so much money had been invested over the previous two years in the entitlement and planning effort. The costs were buried on the balance sheet as an asset.

Even worse, that $1 million had to be written off in one quarter, since the project was "dead." Much to the surprise of the board, the $1 million represented about 15 percent of the company's net worth at the time and, just as suddenly, some of the net worth covenants on bank loans became compromised. Without focusing on the cash going into the planning and approval effort, the financial health of the company was now in danger, particularly with respect to its borrowing capability.

The management of the company had not understood that the "bet"/investment in the new project had the potential of having such a marked negative impact. The lack of both a cash forecast for the company and for the individual project (to show how much cash was going into the planning effort) and a risk analysis of what would happen if the cash invested had to be written off due to a project shutdown had come back to haunt the company.

As a board, we should have seen this defect and counseled the management of the company about taking too many bets on the future, but we were lulled to sleep by the good GAAP financial statements. We did not focus on how much of the asset base consisted of capitalized costs that, if a project had to be abandoned, would quickly deplete the equity of the company through the charge-off of those costs.

Had we insisted on monthly cash flows and projections and pro-forma balance sheets stripped of the capitalized assets, the picture perhaps would have been clearer and the risks would have been more apparent.

Even those of us with deep experience can miss a call and be reminded of a lesson.

In 2007, as the real estate market was continuing to decline, the Verrado master planned community that I was managing near Phoenix was spending nearly $40 million per year on development infrastructure and overhead. Luckily, budgeting was done on a cash basis, and there were good basic tools to track cash in place.

Knowing the importance of cash and cash management, we proactively began to do monthly cash forecasting (rather than the previous quarterly forecast) and to meet with the various departments that were the largest users of cash to begin to understand their needs on a more detailed basis. These meetings, which went from quarterly to monthly, ultimately ended up being weekly meetings.

In the process, not only were uses of cash understood better, but sources that had been ignored before, in good times, were attacked. Reimbursements from utility companies, reconciled receivables, and selling properties that we no longer needed all took on a greater importance as the market declined. The tighter control on expenditures, the heightened focus on getting all kinds of cash in the door, and work on tools that helped to even more accurately forecast cash sources and uses all helped to provide a stronger management of cash at a time when cash was becoming scarcer.

My sense is that by having an existing culture that really was comfortable with cash forecasting, even if it was at a primitive level, helped to get to a more sophisticated management of cash when the situation became more extreme.

The importance of knowing cash, preserving cash, and managing cash all come to the forefront in tough times and remind the manager that, in *all* times, cash is king.

*"Cash is king. GAAP financial statements are nice, but knowing cash flow is critical."*

Exercise: Does your company focus on cash? GAAP statements? Neither? What lessons from this chapter would you apply to your current situation? Why?

_____

_____

_____

_____

_____

_____

_____

_____

_____

_____

_____

_____

_____

_____

_____

_____

_____

_____

_____

_____

_____

# 21

## ALIVE

*In hard times, organizations must adapt to a new and harsh reality or face extinction. The process of staying alive involves tough and personal decisions and actions that can either work toward the long-term benefit of the company or not. Either way, though, an organization has to strive to stay alive.*

In a downturn, companies are faced with stark choices that are oftentimes various shades of awful. Favorite products, traditions, people, or customers may have to be jettisoned in the process of adjusting to a new set of economic realities. The quicker that management teams assess reality and then deal with that reality, the higher the probability of surviving the downturn and living to prosper another day.

The laws of the jungle come into full play in such times.

In good times, our project at Verrado in Arizona enjoyed a quarterly "team-building" day. We would go to a baseball game together or go to a skating rink and have skating, games, and just a social half-day.

It was one of the few times that the entire team of nearly eighty people got to see each other all in one place at the same time.

As the economy worsened, we did not want to give up the quarterly gatherings, but also understood that the $1,000 per quarter allocated to the team building was a truly expendable cost, even if we thought that it was highly important for the group to get together somewhat outside of a full work setting. So we began to get creative in ways to keep the Team Day alive, but to cut the costs of the event.

For example, we did an "Olympic Lunch" around the time of the Beijing Olympic Games. We ordered in Chinese takeout food and had a Nerf javelin contest, an archery contest (with a kid's bow and arrow set), and a discus toss with a Nerf Frisbee. It probably cost $75. The point was that we were still getting together and doing something that was important in keeping the team engaged during a time when there was nothing but bad news. We were just doing it at a significantly scaled-down cost.

The tougher calls are the ones involving people. As the business wound down, we needed fewer people and had to do several rounds of layoffs to adjust the overhead levels to the realities of the revenues we could generate. Even in these decisions and actions, we did them with care and compassion.

Several days before the announcement, we would gather everyone together and explain what was coming, why, and roughly how many people would be involved. On the day of the announcement, we would meet individually with everyone (including those remaining) to either let the person know the terms of their severance or, if they were remaining, how their job might be changing. Afterward, everyone was brought together again and the full group was informed of the changes and the timing of departures.

There was no shunning of the people let go (often times they would stay on for several weeks or months to effect a transition or to finish a project), and all were encouraged to keep their friendships with their co-workers. No one was escorted from the building by a guard. In over a year of multiple rounds of layoffs, nearly every person acted professionally and, even though no one enjoys getting laid off, all understood why and appreciated the dignity of the process. Before each person left, we had a goodbye reception and gave a memento to thank them for their work. It wasn't much, but it was appreciated.

In the process, each team member understood a couple of truths. First was that decisions had to be made to ensure that the business survived. These decisions were never easy, but if people believed that there was a process and that it was a thoughtful process, there was greater acceptance. As the senior manager for the community, I took extraordinary amounts of time to let the team know the realities of what we were dealing with and what the options were. It was not sugar coated, but each felt that he or she was kept in a realistic light rather than in the dark. Second was that dignity was a free commodity and one that had high value to the individual being let go and to those that remained. Although our process probably broke all of the rules of downsizing, it worked for us. Finally, each person was always an ambassador for the company, even if he or she was no longer there. If the story was one of dignified treatment, a thoughtful process, and doing what was necessary for the business to survive, that was not a bad story to have in the community.

The ultimate truth was that if a business does not survive, it cannot do good works in the future. It cannot be a great place for people to work together to do important things that they enjoy doing together. It cannot be an economic engine that helps people to attain their personal goals. It cannot be a contributor to a broader community though volunteer or charitable efforts. It cannot be a contributing part of society.

When times are tough, managers have to do all of the necessary things to ensure that the company has a chance to survive and live to fight another day, even if it means taking steps backward for a while.

## *"Alive is better than dead."*

Exercise: As you have observed company actions in response to an economic downturn, who do you think handled it well? Why? Who did not and why?

_____

_____

_____

_____

_____

_____

_____

_____

_____

_____

_____

_____

_____

_____

_____

_____

_____

_____

_____

_____

_____

# 22

## DOWNSIZING

*When a downturn does arrive, adjusting the organization to a new reality employs all of the lessons learned: have good data, have a bias toward action, and act quickly. The most important lesson of downsizing, though, is to also cut more than you think you need to. It will rarely come back to hurt you.*

Perhaps the most difficult part of a downturn is the decision to eliminate something and, with it, the question of when. Instinct and the natural desire to put off pain works strongly in favor of the status quo. You can't imagine running the business without certain people. Cutting prices could create an issue with customers who had just purchased at the old (usually higher) price and could lead to a negative backlash against the company in the marketplace. Cutting overhead means changing expectations and the ways things have been done.

All of this is disconcerting and easier put off until next week or next month when things might be better (you hope).

However, if the source numbers are good and indicate that cuts are needed, it is almost always better to cut sooner rather than later, and to cut deeper rather than shallower. At the end of nearly every down cycle, those who have dealt with reality and survived will almost always say they wish that they had cut deeper and sooner than they did.

The first time I heard this observation was at an Urban Land Institute conference in San Francisco in the early 1990s. Peter Bedford, a large commercial developer from San Francisco, was relating his experiences with that downturn and his efforts to steer his company through the economic upheaval of the late 1980s and early 1990s. He reviewed the rationale of why he felt that he had to keep certain projects and certain people. Their loyalty or the need to have a tight team for when the market returned were all justifications that he employed. In the end, the projects and the people went anyway, and his cash outflows in supporting both was significant and, ultimately, wasted. Peter's watchword was: "You can't cut too deep too fast."

In this most recent downturn, I remember reminding people of Peter's words as the market began to implode. In the early stages of the downturn, some builders were aggressive in finding what price it took to sell a home and then selling it quickly, if even at a loss. Pulte Homes and D. R. Horton were very good public homebuilders in putting this strategy to work.

Even though they lost money on the sales they made, those who held out longer ultimately got even less and lost even more. This action of finding what the market would bear that day and acting quickly proved to be a winning strategy as soon as the market began to move south. Granted, there were issues with existing customers who had purchased earlier and at higher prices, and talks of lawsuits and such swirled. In the end, though, very few materialized, and those who acted quickly at least stayed alive to fight another day, while those who did not ultimately had to fold their tents.

Similarly, those who were aggressive in cutting their overhead and marketing costs early tended to do better than those who did not. By forcing the organization to adapt to the new realities fast, the pressures of the downturn are mitigated as much as possible.

The risk of the "cut too deep/cut too fast" strategy is that you can go too far. Experience seems to indicate that if expenses or people are cut more than they should be, adding people back (either via consulting arrangements or rehire) or reinstituting programs is a lot less destructive than multiple layers of small cuts dragging over multiple months or quarters. Nearly every manager who has cut quick and deep will come back later and say both it was good to get it over and that there probably could have been more.

All of this experience in a down market leads to the question of how the company got so bloated in the good market. Part is the inertia of growth, part is human nature in creating kingdoms, and part is that organizations left on their own tend to expand what they do without seeing all of the consequences.

Structural limits on organizational size can be attained through hard work and thought. In the late 1990s and early 2000s, I had the opportunity to lead a large team in the completion of the new city of Weston, Florida. The city manager of Weston, John Flint, adopted a unique management philosophy for Weston. He wanted it to be a contract city. Nearly everything would be contracted out: police, fire, finance, park management, etc. In fact, for his first five years, he only had three permanent city employees for a city of over sixty thousand people. Everything else was on contract, and the contracts allowed him to add and reduce staff as the finances and needs of the city adjusted. He didn't have to worry about the politics of laying off "city employees" that seemed to limit what other cities could do.

As times got lean, he was able to more quickly adjust his programs and staffing levels to match his revenue base because of the structure of his organization. While other cities grappled with the tough world of layoffs, Weston adjusted more easily. It is still a fascinating example of a different business model for government that is better.

All a manager has to do is live through one large downsizing in order to be chastened in the next up cycle and be very reluctant to either add people or costs. That is the final lesson of downsizing: watch what you upsize.

Jim Motta, the long-time CEO of Arvida, oftentimes related his experiences in dealing with the downturn of the late 1980s. Arvida, at the time, had a bloated staff and multiple locations. When the downturn hit, Jim had to lay off over two hundred people in one day and shut down many of the offices. As he described it, when the day was done, he stopped at the local store and got a six pack of beer and went to the beach in Boca Raton and promised himself that, when things got better, he would never "staff up" that way again. He stayed true to his word and, when the market did return, Jim ran a very tight ship with very little fat.

There will be a whole new cadre of managers who will be so chastened and will benefit in the next upturn if they remember the lessons of this past downturn.

## *"You can't cut too deep, too fast."*

Exercise: Are there any lessons concerning managing through a downturn that you have learned, either by experience or observation? How would you succinctly state those lessons in a memorable form?

_____

_____

_____

_____

_____

_____

_____

_____

_____

_____

_____

_____

_____

_____

_____

_____

_____

_____

_____

# 23

## CHOICE

*Offering product and feature choice is a strategy to gain market share and increase profits in most businesses. But an inability to execute the flawless delivery of the variety of products created by choice can have the effect of diminishing profits and repelling customers. How you organize is the key to success for this strategy.*

Homes are complicated things to build. The number of "things" that go together to make a home can number into the thousands. Each of those "things," in turn, has multiple alternatives to choose from: different manufacturers, different designs, different specifications, different dimensions, and so forth.

Anyone who has walked the aisles of Home Depot or Lowe's and just looked at the array of bathroom faucets on display gets an opportunity to look at the tip of the iceberg. What the mass-market home retailers carry in stock and display is but a small fraction of the possibilities that are out there. Trying to decide what items to choose from as a builder of new homes can be daunting, and the process leads to multiple business models.

For example, custom builders who permit their customers the broadest array of choice for items in their home can satisfy the customers' desire to "have exactly what they want." A custom porcelain lavatory sink from France? Perhaps a sauna from Finland? The price for that unfettered choice is usually high cost, slow production time, extensive rework, and, often, impaired customer satisfaction. Even though the goal of letting customers choose whatever they want is to ultimately satisfy them, oftentimes the process of doing so creates such stress that the end result is unsatisfied customers and endless cocktail stories of the horrors of building a custom home.

On the other hand, not offering any choice at all also has its issues. By predetermining the product and all of its components up front, manufacturing costs and speeds can be managed tightly and predictably, and customers who desire exactly that product are most often satisfied. However, those who do not exactly want the product have to compromise if they purchase the product. They, too, can be dissatisfied, but for different reasons than the custom buyer.

American manufacturing has run the gamut of these two extremes. Ford's Model "T" offered any color you wanted, as long as it was black. Apple's iPod comes in multiple sizes with multiple colors and multiple memory size alternatives. The iPhone, iPads, iTouches, Shuffle, and iPod all do similar things, but are targeted to different consumer segments.

So which business model is best? Offering a lot of choice or offering little choice?

This question continues to appear as managers try to decide what strategies to pursue. Some general rules tend to apply, though. First, the lower the selling price, the more palatable no or minimal choice becomes. The higher the price, the more the buyer tends to want choice in their purchase decision. Generally, though, choice is better than no choice, and the question then becomes one of how much choice is enough. When given the option, customers will usually go for choice, if the price is the same.

The corollary question then becomes one of whether the company is organized to flawlessly deliver the choice alternatives that it will offer. The only thing worse than not offering choice is to offer it and then fail miserably in the process of delivering the choice (see "Organizations tend to do the things they are organized to do"). However, by effectively offering and delivering choice, a company can develop a premium for its product and generate superior margins in the process.

In the late 1990s I served as the president of Arvida's South Florida operations building the Weston community. Our prime business was the development of a ten-thousand-acre, sixteen-thousand-home "new town," about twenty miles west of Fort Lauderdale. Arvida was somewhat unique in that it was both the community developer (doing all the roads, utilities, parks, schools, etc.) and the sole production home-builder in the community. We had about twelve different "product lines" offered at any one time. They ranged from condominiums and townhomes all the way to semicustom homes on acre lots in a country club setting. Each "product line" had between three and six different house styles (one and two story; three, four, five bedrooms, etc.). In turn, each house style had between three and six different "elevations" or architectural looks offered. There were between three and six approved color schemes that could be applied to those elevations.

And that was just the primary level of complexity.

In order to present an interesting streetscape, no two similar homes could be next to one another or across the street from a similar style home. All of this was done to service a broad swath of the marketplace in order to attain the high sales volumes (in excess of one thousand homes per year) needed to support the high levels of infrastructure costs necessary to create a totally new community.

Once the "what house on what lot" determinations were made, the customer had the opportunity to then select options and "colors" inside of his or her home.

For several years, the business model at Weston had been one where buyers of less expensive homes were given little or no choice of options (different appliances, light fixtures, additional outlets and switches, upgraded trim packages, etc.) and a limited selection of colors for cabinets, tile, carpets, countertops, and so forth. Buyers of the more expensive homes were allowed to have multiple choices and oftentimes brought in "custom" selections that had to be researched and purchased.

Interestingly, when we started to review both profitability and customer satisfaction by product segment ("In God we trust; all others bring data"), the profit margins (as a percentage) on the more customized homes were less than those on the lower priced homes with fewer selections and the customer satisfaction for the buyers of the more expensive homes was significantly lower than that of the buyers of the more standardized product. In both cases, though, the margins were at the lower end of industry comparatives and the customer satisfaction had significant potential upside also.

We could do better was the conclusion.

After a complete evaluation of our business model, which had customers making their option and color selections in small "selection rooms" and doing their selections multiple times through the construction process), we chose to organize differently.

We decided to open a thirty-thousand-square-foot design center that displayed options and selections in a highly professional retail setting that was open daily for prospective customer introduction, customer orientation, and customer selections. We also set up a separate team to manage the options and design center and ran it as an integrated business unit. The team had the ability to condense and standardize the selections and to offer them across all products. Even though the inexpensive home buyers would probably not buy the high-end dishwasher, they could choose it if they wanted to. Few did.

Our feeling was that, since all buyers did their option selections in the same place, they had to have the "run of the house." The team organized to understand what various market segments typically wanted and had pre-priced option packages that contained most of the popular items, if the customer wanted to go the easy way.

They dealt daily with the purchasing group and the subcontractor base to gain detailed knowledge of the products so that they could best inform the customer of the features and benefits of each choice. They shopped not only our competitors, but the big-box retailers to know competitive pricing. It was a full business approach.

In the process, we were able to offer more of the simple upgrades for our lower-priced products, and we limited what we offered to the higher-end buyers to those things we knew we could get from our suppliers and for which we knew our costs up front.

By coupling the design center with a firm policy of not allowing any choices that were not shown in the design center and requiring all choices to be made prior to the commencement of construction, we created a business model that allowed us both fast cycle times and reasonable margins. Our option sales per home increased over 20 percent, the margins went up by nearly a quarter, and our customer satisfaction for the process went from under 80 percent to over 97 percent in less than two years.

By spending a lot of time up front explaining the rules and the process to potential customers, we also weeded out customers who did not want to purchase under those conditions. This was a hard sell initially for our sales group, but it quickly discovered that the customers who bought into the whole program were more satisfied and more likely to refer. The customers from before who wanted to truly customize were not accommodated in this model, but, in the end, they proved to be a very small segment of the buyer pool that also tended to chew up immense amounts of sales time and were highly inclined to sue.

The bottom line was that offering choice, but structured choice that fit a business model of our choosing, was better than both no choice at all and unlimited choice. Reorganizing ourselves differently to deliver choice allowed us to succeed.

> *"Choice is better than no choice, as long as you are organized to deliver the choices that are offered."*

Exercise: What company in your experience offers a high degree of choice and does it well? Why? How about a company that attempts to offer choice and fails? Why do you think they fail?

_____

_____

_____

_____

_____

_____

_____

_____

_____

_____

_____

_____

_____

_____

_____

_____

_____

_____

_____

_____

# 24

## VALUE

*The essence of a profitable business is to deliver value in excess of cost. A physical product can provide value to a customer. However, intangibles can provide value, too, and the most powerful of these involves the ability to connect people to one another easily, so that they can be part of a larger community.*

Since 1998, I have been involved with the development of master planned communities in Florida, the Carolinas, Colorado, California, and Arizona. When one is involved with the creation of new towns or cities that involve residential, commercial, educational, recreational, and institutional uses, you get a very different view of value and how people interpret and pay for value.

As a homebuilder for over twenty-five years, I saw a narrow slice of how people valued their home and the broader place they lived. In the home itself, people valued the kinds of spaces you provided to them: the size of the lot, the design of the home (both inside and out), the quality and types of finishes and appliances you installed, the overall quality of the workmanship, and how well they were treated before, during, and after the sale. These were relatively easy things to create and control.

You could use market research to determine what the hot buttons and key features were for a target demographic profile, and, by providing a reasonable level of choice and flexibility, you could tailor the home to a relatively diverse market segment. By controlling the business practices and the morale of your staff, you could influence greatly the customer's experience. If you did the two excellently (a great home that hit all the customer's hot buttons and a positive experience for the customer), you had a good business and made money.

However, the creation and delivery of a home was relatively easy to do, and homes quickly become commodities, selling by the square foot, more often than not. The commoditization of homes eventually deteriorates profit margins as competitors cut prices and customers begin to look at one home being the same as the next.

I also knew that not all homes are created equal. You could build the same twenty-eight-hundred-square-foot colonial home in Lawrenceville and in Princeton two adjacent communities in central New Jersey, and the home in Princeton would sell for double (or more) the price of the same home in Lawrenceville. The impact of community, beyond the actual features of the home, had a marked impact on value. The quality of schools, the services available to town residents, and the type of neighbors you met all had an impact on value and the price that people were willing to pay. The price differential attributable to the town that you were in and the neighborhood or part of town your house was located in was oftentimes greater than the value of the physical home itself.

This holds true no matter where you live in the country. There are always places that are more preferred than others, and people are willing to pay more for that difference.

As a creator of new communities, the question was: which factors provided the highest ratio of value to cost? If you could provide those intangible factors, your community would be more valuable, and that value could be cashed in, either through higher land prices or higher sales velocities, or both. This applied both to the initial sale of the home and also to subsequent re-sales. If the residents and their elected officials kept the value differentiators alive, the value for all residents was enhanced for a very long time.

I had learned that master planned communities oftentimes tried to create the incremental value through the creation of amenities: golf courses, tennis facilities, walking trails, parks, etc. These physical facilities are expensive to build and are also expensive to maintain, as I have learned over the years. They provide a good "buzz" in initial marketing efforts and, as long as someone else is footing the bill for running and maintaining them, residents tend to love them. Who wouldn't? It was a luxury you did not have to fully pay for.

However, when the true cost of ownership inevitably becomes evident, many users are reluctant to pay it, leaving the true long-term value to the smaller group that is willing to pay. Ultimately, the amenities become a small-business enterprise that has to compete for discretionary dollars from households in the community.

In the process of managing and creating new communities, however, a second form of amenity started to reveal itself to me. This amenity, rooted less in physical product, involved the entities and programs that brought people together to interact with each other. These programs were based upon a common affinity. They still required some physical facility or venue to "happen," but the "fanciness" of the facility was less important than the programs themselves and the relationships developed and nurtured by the programs.

I grew up in Cohasset, Massachusetts, a small town of about three thousand residents about twenty-five miles south of Boston. It was a town that went back to the mid-1600s and was the classic New England town with white clapboard houses and white clapboard churches arrayed around a "common" in the center of town.

There was a women's club that my mother and grandmother belonged to that met every month. There was a garden club, too. There was a Memorial Day parade, a Fourth of July fireworks display, a Veteran's Day parade, a carnival on the common every June, a parade for the opening of Little League season, an American Legion, a Veterans of Foreign Wars, a volunteer firemen's group, and on and on. Each of these events or groups had a structure around it, and people became involved, some more seriously than others.

The women's club had officers and put on programs every month with guest speakers and a luncheon. So did the garden club. It had an annual garden tour that raised money for charity. I am sure that there was a degree of crossover of the members of both clubs, but there were also some interested in one, but not the other.

What I do know is that if you worked with someone on a program for the garden club and then saw that same person at a Little League game and then again at the high school band concert and again at church, that familiarity made you feel part of the overall community. It provided an opportunity to have friendships. It also provided an opening for developing a connection to the community at large and, over time, the opportunity to contribute in whatever way was appropriate for your circumstances.

The events and clubs and traditions were the ways that residents connected to one another, and those connections provided the glue that bound the community together generation after generation. When new folks moved in, it was a vehicle to begin to connect to your new neighbors and become a part of the community at large. It was part of what made the community valuable, and that value was reflected in the real estate prices of the town as a whole.

Similarly, the town had a great school system. Through hard work by teachers and parents, a high percentage of the graduates went on to college, even those from families where no one had gone to college before. The schools provided another venue for residents to get together and work on things together. Being part of the PTA, volunteering as a teacher's aide, working the snack stand at football games, and supporting school efforts financially were all ways for town residents to connect with one another, create friendships, and, in the process, work on another driver of value: a great school system.

In a newer community, all of those structures do not necessarily exist and have to be created from scratch. Although they may happen organically, if a developer helps to induce their creation, they tend to occur more quickly. In doing so, the value of these intangibles can be recognized sooner, while the community is still being developed and the developer can partake in some of that value creation.

For example, at the Weston community in south Florida, Arvida, the developer, had created a Memorial Day race. The race (a 5k run and a 5k walk) was initially started as a holiday event so that the community, in its infant days, could meet and interact with their neighbors, in a broad sense. It also helped to market the homes and lots in the community by providing a venue for prospective customers to see what it was like to live in Weston and to meet people who might be their neighbors.

After the event, there was a cookout, and it provided a structure for people to come together. Initially, volunteers helped the developer to organize the race and events. As businesses began to develop in the community, civic and business organizations (chambers of commerce, Rotary, Lions, etc.) began to evolve and be created also. The melding of an organization looking to have a community outreach and an event that needed a long-term sponsor and guardian became a natural, and the race eventually became the charge of the new local Rotary Club.

On a separate occasion, a group of three or four pet owners approached us to see if they could work on a program to celebrate pets and pet owners. With very little seed money (less than $3,000 in the first year), "Pets and Pals in the Park" was launched with events like a dog parade, Frisbee catching, and an owner-pet look-alike contest. With several hundred participants in the first year, the event grew and became self-sustaining through sponsorships from IAMS, veterinarians, and local businesses. It provided a community leadership outlet for a group of people who both loved their pets and wanted to spend their time with other like-minded folks. When potential customers, who were also pet owners, visited the community and found out that there was a place for them, the decision to buy in the community was a lot easier.

As these structures and lessons became clearer, I recognized that there was an underlying social value that was being satisfied through this "social infrastructure." The one thing that people have in common when they move to a new place is that they know nearly no one. They are islands in a sea of unknowns. To the extent that there are readily available organizations and programs that provide easy opportunities to become involved in the community and to meet other residents, there is a greater chance of developing friends and beginning to "fit in."

This was different in very significant ways from having a nice house that met your every dream but didn't offer any easy way to meet your neighbors. It also made houses less of a commodity. Other homes that were in a communities or subdivisions that did not have the kind of "social infrastructure" that a Weston can provide were at a severe disadvantage. The people who lived in Weston were in a "bubble" where the intangibles helped to both increase and protect their residential value.

For lack of any other descriptor, I noted that there seemed to be "a high value to the elimination of loneliness." When people could satisfy this need to connect and not be as lonely as they might have been, they were willing to pay more for their home in such a community. More people were willing to buy in a place that had these structures (clubs, events, churches, etc.), and businesses were more willing to set up shop in a place where they could be more than a store in the strip mall; they could be part of a community, too.

In trying to test what this value was worth, it appeared to be a premium of between 10 percent and 20 percent above homes and communities which did not have social infrastructure. Since a builder typically only makes a 6 percent to 10 percent profit margin, that is a lot of money.

I had the opportunity to speak on the topic of social infrastructure to a gathering of the Urban Land Institute in New York in the early 2000s. It was before this group that I first used the phrase "high value to the elimination of loneliness" in a public setting, and the room went still. Later, several developers and marketers came up and said that they had never put all of the pieces together that way.

Facilities without programming were hollow shells, but programming, even with the most rudimentary of facilities, was a game changer in terms of value creation for the developer, value preservation and enhancement for residents, and lifestyle enhancement for residents. That is a true win-win.

At the time, there was no such thing as Facebook, Twitter, LinkedIn, or other social networking sites. However, if you look at their explosive growth of these "social networking" sites across multiple age groups and demographics in the past couple of years, it is pretty obvious to me that they have found the same basic truth that I found when it came to physical community development.

## *"There is high value to the elimination of loneliness."*

Exercise: What companies seem to deliver high value? What enables them to do it? What companies fail to deliver value and why?

_____

_____

_____

_____

_____

_____

_____

_____

_____

_____

_____

_____

_____

_____

_____

_____

_____

_____

_____

# 25

## KIDS AND RATIONALITY

*Parents will go to great lengths to potentially enable a better life for their children. Whether it is through education, sports, or some form of the arts, parents will do things and spend money in a seemingly irrational way seeking a potential advantage for their child's future. In business, if that urge is understood and that tendency tapped, value can be created.*

I have two children: both sons and both grown. After the journey from their birth to their introduction to the working world after college, I have developed a perspective on parenting that is probably pretty mainstream in its thoughts.

I believe that most parents are "hard-wired" to do everything they can for their children to do well in the world and, ideally, to improve upon whatever station or accomplishment the parents have achieved.

Children are also little avatars of the parents. They are where parents sometimes play out their frustrations, desires, hopes, and social standing with other parents. One cannot go to a children's sporting event without noticing how some parents are "into it" way more than the kids are. They live and die with each accomplishment and failure of the child in a manner that is disproportionate to the actual import of the match.

This competitive streak plays itself out on sports fields, in classrooms, in dance recitals, in scout troops, in church choirs, and at summer camps. Sometimes it is healthy and sometimes it is not. Without doubt it occurs in so many venues that it must be considered to be part of human nature, rather than an anomaly, at least here in the United States.

Attendant to this competition, in many cases, is a parental drive to try to ensure that the education that their children receive is the best possible. Parents will try to live in towns and cities that offer the best public educational opportunities and results on a consistent basis. They will stretch their incomes to try to live in those towns at the expense of other uses of their incomes

On a more micro scale, it plays out in the teachers their children have and the politics of those assignments. Every edge is considered, along with how that edge might impact the child's educational performance and his or her ultimate ability to gain acceptance into the best college possible. There is a firm belief (sometimes proven, sometimes disproven) that the quality and "pecking order" of college will determine the future earning capacity of that child, along with the "quality" of his or her lifelong friends and, perhaps, his or her eventual mate.

The connection path between which neighborhood one lives in, what kindergarten teacher the child has, and how he or she is doing in beginning reading, to eventual college matriculation, financial success, and social standing, is a very real one for many parents. Even one deviation off the line can seem catastrophic to those so focused on the roadmap to apparent success.

As a new community developer, an understanding of this dynamic is important in helping to create the value of a community and its real estate. The quality and choice of schools in a community are two of the most important determinants in a buying decision for families with school-age children. Even for those without children, good schools can improve resale value, because the market broadens to families with school-age children in a resale situation.

One can look at existing communities in the country, and those with the highest property values often correlate with the ability of the schools to consistently produce high SAT scores and placements into the most selective colleges. Home buyers with children will often trade off house size and amenities in order to be able to live in a community with a great school system.

It becomes a self-fulfilling dynamic. Parents who value education tend to become more involved in the school system and its activities, and that involvement tends to both bring in better teachers and to keep better teachers in that system. That stability, in turn, allows for the development of a positive culture that is a key driver to educational performance. And all of that brings in more parents who value education.

As a developer of new communities, none of this is in existence when you start, and so the problem becomes one of how to create the system that leads to high property values driven by great schools. The formula is fairly complex, but it most often involves an early partnership between the developer and whatever the local school governing authority may be. In this partnership, the developer arranges for schools to be built early in the community's life and for enhancement programs for both teacher training and curriculum enhancement to be available. This is done sometimes through the state's colleges of teacher education and other times through private foundations. In any event, the key element becomes an ability to influence the hiring of great principals who can attract strong teachers and are able to set a positive culture from the beginning.

It is hard work, and expensive, too. Front-ending schools, curriculum enhancements, and helping to establish the cultural, leadership, and training systems for a new set of schools can run into the millions and tens of millions of dollars before they pay off in accelerated sales and higher land values, but the return on investment can be north of 30 percent, compounded.

Even if a new community is not being developed, the insight that parents do irrational things for their children still applies. Whether it is parents moving to a neighborhood or town because of the superior youth lacrosse, soccer, swimming, or other sports programs or moving to a neighborhood in order to be in the boundary for consideration for a certain parochial school, decisions are driven by a parent's choice of spending time and/or money in order to create an advantage for his or her kids. What seems irrational at first is highly rational to parents living inside of a value system.

I saw this impact first hand. In the development of the Weston community in south Florida, Arvida had school excellence as one of the cornerstones of the community that ultimately grew to nearly sixteen thousand homes and a population of over sixty-five thousand.

Working first with elementary and middle schools, the community developed a reputation for having some of the best schools in south Florida. Families valuing education that moved to south Florida always had Weston near the top of their list. Because Florida is based upon county-based school administration, control of who attended the schools was not necessarily vested in the community. People from outside of the neighborhood could apply to have their children attend a school and, theoretically, if there were vacancies, they could. In reality, people became creative and would list their children with addresses of "relatives" who did live in the community. Oftentimes the "relatives" would charge about $500 per year per child to vouch for the child living at their address.

This reached its extreme when the on-location high school for the community was built near the end of the development of Weston. Children from Weston had gone to a high school adjacent to, but outside of, Weston that served Weston as well as several neighboring communities. Designed for about twenty-five hundred kids, it had nearly five thousand jammed into portables, gyms, and storage rooms. The new Weston High School was designed for twenty-eight hundred ninth- through twelfth-graders. We had tracked the school-age population in Weston and knew with a high degree of certainty that there would be about twenty-two hundred high-school-age children from the community, of which between 10 percent and 20 percent would go off to private, parochial, or boarding schools, so twenty-eight hundred would be more than enough to service the community with room left for growth.

In its first year of operation, the school opened with just ninth through eleventh grades (the five hundred or so twelfth-graders would remain at their old high school to finish their senior year). The new high school opened with about twenty-two hundred children, and by the end of the school year was up over twenty-eight hundred. When it reopened with all four grades a year later, it was at about thirty-five hundred and overcrowded.

We knew the kids were not coming from the community; we had a nearly perfect census of family composition. The traffic jam every day showed cars coming from Dade County (Weston was in Broward County). What we discovered was a deep underground economy of parents dissatisfied with schools in Dade County and in other parts of Broward County that were beyond the Weston High School boundary. They had found an entrepreneurial group inside of Weston that "rented" its address and was making its housing payments with the proceeds from the "rent" that allowed kids from outside of the community to attend the preferred school.

The last time I checked, the Weston High School had gone over four thousand, was highly overcrowded, and the "old" high school had shrunk to around two thousand kids. When given anything that looked like a free economy, parents were willing to pay, cheat, and lie to try to get their kids away from their existing school and into one that was better, either in reality or in perception.

They were willing to work through an underground economy to drive up to an hour each way each day in order to have a better opportunity for their children. Similarly, many families were willing to pay the 15 percent to 30 percent premium that houses in Weston commanded to the marketplace in order to have a preferred environment for education for their kids.

To some it may seem irrational, but, in fact, that is the lesson. The apparent irrationality was eminently rational to the parents when seen through the prism of parents trying to do anything they can to create an advantage for their children.

This observation applies outside of the real estate world as well as inside of it. Just look at when a hot toy hits the market and parents fight to get it for their kids before it flies off the shelf. Or look how parents in New York City maneuver, network, and sometimes connive to get their kids into the "right" kindergarten that will only cost them $25,000 per year, plus donations to the annual fund. There are prep courses for four- and five-year-olds as they go into the interview process for these cherished spots, and those prep courses can cost in the thousands of dollars.

Carry it forward to summer sports camps run by college coaches to whom parents would like to introduce their potential next quarterback, and the list continues in the same vein.

By understanding that parents will go to extremes for their child's future and then learning how to build that "irrationality" into a business proposition, a company can create value far beyond the value of its physical product.

*"Parents will do irrational things for their kids."*

Exercise: Are there any other apparent truisms regarding parents and children that you have observed? What would they be?

_____

_____

_____

_____

_____

_____

_____

_____

_____

_____

_____

_____

_____

_____

_____

_____

_____

_____

_____

# 26

## FREQUENCY

*Improving productivity is an important part of improving value. A key part of improving productivity is the frequency with which a manager reviews how production is running compared to expectations (schedule). More frequent review allows deviations to be spotted sooner and corrections made more quickly, leading to fewer defects, less "down-time," and higher productivity.*

When I first started to manage homebuilding projects, the regular routine was to update the schedule once a week. Updating the schedule meant that the superintendent would check off the stages of construction that were completed on each house during the prior week. Sometimes it was done on Monday morning and sometimes on Friday afternoon. Sometimes the work was checked off as complete even if minor "punch list" items remained and the subcontractor had to come back to actually completely finish the work.

By the time I got the updated schedule, it was Tuesday or Wednesday of the next week, and then I would discuss any delays with the superintendent.

The information by that time was nearly a week old, and any problems had, most likely, been rectified by the passage of time. Of course, any new problems that were occurring would not show up until the next report.

Only if an activity remained undone for more than a week did it rise to the category of a problem to be addressed. This was not an atypical system in the building business in the 1970s and 1980s, and it was not uncommon for it to take six months or more to build a house.

In the mid-1990s, as I became more involved in Total Quality Management and process improvement efforts, the issues of productivity and efficiency began to rise in importance in my mind. When we began to look at activities in an individual home, the most likely situation was that no one was in the home working.

Activities tended to happen with great effort at the beginning of the week, but by the end of the week, houses would be deserted. It seemed that superintendents had simple scheduling systems whereby they would call the subcontractor over the weekend and set up his work for the next week, always endeavoring to get the work done early in the week. This left time at the end of the week in case the trade partner didn't show up or needed to come back because he was unable to finish the work at the time that he was initially scheduled.

With a superintendent handling between fifteen and thirty homes at any one time, this system was the best that many companies could do and still stay alive and sane. It was not efficient, though. The interest meter did not stop when no one was in the house, and customers would be constantly nagging the superintendent about why no one was working on their house.

With the advent of computerized scheduling programs, such as Microsoft Project and PrimaVera, the hand work involved in scheduling began to disappear. With a scheduling template in hand and critical path logics built into scheduling programs, it became easier to schedule work. Similarly, the advent of e-mail, cellular phones, and Web-based applications made the ability to communicate with trade partners easier.

However, it became increasingly obvious that the scheduling programs were only as good as the frequency with which they were updated and the accuracy of the information in the update. When deviations did appear, the ability to quickly devise a course of action to correct the deviation and get the project back on course again was highly important.

The first element, frequency of update, was critical. If you were ever going to manage a problem, having current information was necessary. In homes, where the frequency of update had been weekly, the time period changed to daily (and, as efficiency became better, actually to the half-day). In site improvement work, where the update had been weekly or at the time of completion of phases, daily updates became a requirement also. Only by having current information could the deviations to schedule be spotted and corrective actions taken quickly enough so that the schedule delays were minimized.

The old adage of "garbage in, garbage out" comes into play, too. The information that is used to update the schedule had to be perfectly correct in order to paint an accurate picture of what was happening. The old system of marking an item complete, when in fact there were punch list items remaining, had to be revised.

Finally, having a system in place to track deviations from schedule regularly and manage the corrective action was needed. This involved a daily (and sometimes twice a day) gathering of a team designated to handle items that had gone "off schedule" and to rectify the situation, coordinating solutions with the superintendent and the trade contractor involved.

By also analyzing data from these defects, persistent issues could be identified and resolved so that root causes of delays could be systematically eliminated.

This system led to an understanding that if you managed things by the month, you could wait as long as a month to figure out what was wrong and then begin to take corrective action. Similarly, if you managed by the week, you would have to wait a week in order to figure out what was wrong and then begin corrections. The same applies to managing by the day and by the hour.

In each case, the longer you waited to get information on out-of-schedule or out-of-process events, the more time was lost until you could begin to correct whatever was wrong.

In this world, understanding the inherent speed of the process becomes important. In building a home, managing by the day or half-day is about the right frequency. If you were managing an assembly line creating one thousand widgets per hour, more frequent monitoring (by the hour or by the minute) might be called for.

In the homebuilding operations at the Weston community, the problem became magnified. By 2000, we had ramped up the production of homes to twenty-five per week, or over 1,250 per year. At any one time, we were managing over six hundred homes in various stages of production (prestart, under construction, completed, and awaiting closing), and the logistics of keeping track of the work, scheduling it, finding and correcting problems, and ensuring quality were significant.

Luckily, the small team of senior managers that I had brought with me to Florida when I had accepted the assignment to manage Weston had been working on adapting the PrimaVera scheduling program for use in tracking multiple houses under construction.

Using techniques we had developed previously, the scheduling program was up and running in 1999 after about six months.

The harder part of the conversion was training the superintendents (about thirty-five of them) in a different way to manage. They had to be diligent about noting early in the day whether the scheduled trade partners had arrived to do their work for the day. If they had not, we developed a specialized team that worked on that problem so the superintendent could focus on the management of the work in the houses that day, rather than trying to track down a missing trade partner.

Similarly, at the end of the day, the superintendent had to note the status of the work for each house and whether it was completed or not. That information was then delivered to a data clerk who updated the data in the PrimaVera program and re-ran the master schedule that was automatically e-mailed to each trade that evening, giving the work for the next day and the upcoming two weeks. (This was before the time when tablets and PDAs were easily synched to software and before the time that schedules could be posted to the Web.)

Once the superintendents saw that the daily management of the information was paying off in fewer problems on the site, they began to buy in. The change was harder for them because their job had changed. The old yelling and bullying that had characterized the classic behavior of the "gruff old superintendent" was now replaced by having to know the schedule, manage the trades in their houses, and focus on solving problems as they occurred during the day.

The trade partners bought in sooner because the data they got was faster and better, and this allowed them to operate much more efficiently.

Even though the number of homes being managed was significant, the cycle time for building homes dropped. In our case, the conversion to managing by the day allowed us to cut our home construction time from over 180 calendar days to less than half of that number. This more than doubled our return on assets.

Working on scheduling is nearly free, but the results can be stunning.

The key was being able to manage by the day with good data.

## *"Manage by the day, get results by the day."*

Exercise: Are there any generalizations that you have with regard to how intensely things should be managed? What would they be?

_____

_____

_____

_____

_____

_____

_____

_____

_____

_____

_____

_____

_____

_____

_____

_____

_____

_____

_____

_____

_____

_____

# 27

## MINDING YOUR P'S

*When confronting a marketing-based problem in your business, it is help-ful to use the structure of the "7 P's" to help evaluate your business or of-fering against that of your competition. Reviewing Product, Price, Place, Promotion, People, Process, and Presentation will usually lead to areas for possible improvement. Of the seven, the People "P" is oftentimes the most critical in achieving successful change and improvement.*

No matter what business you are in, the fundamen-tals are really the same. You have a product, a market, a competitive environment, and a set of economics. Hopefully, your business model allows the business to deliver its product or products at a price that is in excess of its costs, thereby creating a profit. Ideally the profit provides a reasonable financial return com-pared to the capital invested in the business.

Whether it is houses, cellular telephones, jet air-planes, legal services, or selling lemonade on the cor-ner, the basics stay relatively fixed.

In crafting a new business, adding a new busi-ness line, or trying to figure out how to retool an underperforming business, having a roadmap for attacking the problem can be very helpful. Over the years, I have found that using a system called the 7 P's provides such a roadmap.

For me, the 7 P's had their genesis in a marketing course I took at Wharton. Don Blankhertz, the long-time marketing professor, wrote one of the seminal marketing texts of the time that was the basis of the MBA Marketing 101 course. In the book, his organizing principle is that the basics of marketing could be boiled down to four elements: product, price, place, and promotion. It was a pretty easy checklist to remember and I tucked it away. Long after recalling what was said in detail in the book, the 4 P's remained.

In the spirit of fair disclosure, the structure of the four P's is credited to Professor Neil Borden of the Harvard Business School, who first started to use the phrase in 1949 and wrote about it in 1964.

As I began to work on business problems in the real world, both as a consultant and as a builder/developer, a common set of problems kept arising involving marketing. We would have a housing subdivision that was underperforming or a house in the lineup that was not selling. These situations presented a challenge to try to figure out why and then how to correct the situation.

The 4 P's provided at least the beginning of a simple checklist. How did the product stack up against the competition? How was our price and value proposition compared to our competitors'? Was our location better or worse? How were our advertising and promotional efforts compared to our competitors?

Quickly I found that there were some other factors that seemed to weigh in the evaluation and, by the late 1980s, the list began to expand to become what I called the 7 P's of Good Marketing:

- Product
- Price
- Place
- Promotion
- People
- Process
- Presentation

(In the process of writing and researching this book, I have found that others also developed "7 P" lists for a variety of industries. In 2004, an article by Brian Tracy ("The 7 P's of Marketing"), notes the P's as being Product, Price, Promotion, Place, Packaging, Positioning, and People. A separate article by Karl Sultana ("Understanding the 7 Ps of Marketing"), describes the 7 Ps as Product, Price, Placement, Promotion, People, Process, and Physical Evidence. It is interesting that different observers and analysts seem to always come with the total of seven, but the description of the P's differs slightly depending upon the viewpoint of the author.)

By evaluating the situation in both a qualitative and a quantitative manner by comparing these factors for our product or service compared to a competitor's, usually areas of improvement could be identified and the beginnings of an action plan developed.

When looking at new projects or products, thinking about the checklist allowed us to position well in a marketplace, also. It forced a rigorous evaluation of strengths and weaknesses. Some things just couldn't be changed easily (for example, once a housing subdivision had been purchased, changing the physical location component of Place was impossible), while others were fairly flexible (Price, for example).

Here are some basic thoughts around these seven items.

**Product:**   This should include both the physical and nonphysical product (service) you are delivering. For example, when doing a housing community, the product consisted of the characteristics of the neighborhood (parks, walking trails, etc.), the actual house, the services provided in the transaction (warranty, concierge, interior design help, etc.), and the true intangibles of the community (ease of meeting others through clubs and events). Together they provide the product the customer is purchasing. If your product was a smart phone, such as an iPhone or a Blackberry, the evaluation would include the physical design of the phone, the design and utility of the software, the cell network(s) that the phone works on, the service for the phone, etc.

**Price:**   Pretty simple; this is what you pay. However, it should also include the elements of how you pay. For example, if the price includes extended terms or a higher commission rate to a broker or finder, these factors have to be weighed also.

**Place:**   This is a little more complicated. In the real estate world, this consists of both the macro and micro locations of the real estate (what city, what part of town, what neighborhood, what the experience is in getting there, etc.). For service businesses, this would involve the location of your office, the environment that surrounds you, etc. For products, it would involve the locations where your customers interact with your product as part of their information gathering and/

or purchase experience. In the virtual world, place is the look, feel, and presence of your Web site. In some industrial applications, the distribution channel and its effectiveness are factors in the place conversation.

**Promotion:** This factor encompasses all of the ways that potential customers learn about your product or service, from advertising to public relations to customer recommendations to social networking.

**People:** This was the first of my additions to Blankhertz's 4 P's. The importance of the people element and their interaction with customers consistently came up as I evaluated marketing performance. Great salespeople could overcome deficiencies in a lot of the other P's and have higher levels of sales, drive higher profits, and create higher customer satisfaction. On the other hand, having all of the other P's right, but in the hands of weak or offensive salespeople, always gave substandard results. From the importance of face-to-face salespeople to the importance of who you speak with on the telephone for a service call, measuring and quantifying the people component from the eyes of the customer is very critical.

**Process:** This was the second addition to Blankhertz's list. The more I studied quality and process improvement, the more I began to understand how the process that the customer went through to learn about, purchase, and receive service for your product was a critical piece that had to be considered. If it is easy to get information and to make a purchase, it has a value in a customer's eyes and impacts the overall value equation. Understanding the experience that a customer has with your business impacts the willingness to refer positively as well as the immediate purchase decision. Learning to quantify this experience and compare it to your competitors is a valuable exercise for any company.

**Presentation:** This was the final addition. Presentation involves how your product looks to the customer and the impressions about value and quality that are conveyed. In the real estate world, this would involve the cleanliness of a community or a house, the entry landscape experience of a community, the decoration of the sales office and demonstration homes, the look and feel of a Web site and collateral printed materials, the dress of anyone the customer may come in contact with, the cleanliness of a salesperson's car, etc. For a retail product, it might be the display in a store, the packaging of the product, the smell or touch or feel of the product, and the dress of salespeople who are selling the product.

I am sure that there could be other elements of review. The importance here, though, is that the simplicity of the list of the 7 P's allows a manager to have both a simple evaluation tool and one that can be easily taught to others. And that, in itself, is worth something.

When I was at Realen Homes (near Philadelphia) in the early 1990s, we began to actively include the 7 P's in our community marketing reviews, which occurred three times per year. In the reviews, the project team (a project manager, the construction superintendent, and the site sales manager) would look at their project's performance and compare it against what they had done previously, what our other projects were doing, and against their nearby competition.

The superintendent would be focusing on quality metrics, the cycle time of production, performance of trade partners, and so forth. The sales manager would be looking at the competitive marketplace and how our sales prices, sales rates, customer satisfaction, and market share metrics held up, along with the strength of our floor plans. The project manager would be involved in these analyses, plus would be looking at financial performance for the project and overall project strategy.

Together, based upon this review, they would develop a set of recommendations for action and improvement and then present the review and recommendations to a senior management team. The senior managers would challenge, evaluate, and, together with the team, develop an action plan for the community.

It was a very effective system that relied on data and team collaboration to move the project forward.

As the overall market began to turn down in the early 1990s, the competition became fierce between builders, and oftentimes sales rates slipped.

Realen had a community in Buckingham, Pennsylvania, about an hour north of Philadelphia, that began to run into issues. Its sales rates began to slip. Even though production quality seemed to be high, the customer satisfaction ratings were beginning to slip also. When compared to the overall market and our competition, which were also slipping, our deterioration seemed to be proportionately more.

The project team believed that our prices were too high, our homes too large, and our incentives were not enough to close deals. The sales manager, who had prospered with the company throughout the good times, believed that if we changed those elements (Product, Price, and Promotion), we would get our competitive position back.

Both the project team and senior management felt that our location (Place) was as good as or better than our competition's. Our site was significantly cleaner and more organized. Our process for writing contracts, doing selections, and interacting with customers was again equal to or better than others (Process). Our decorated models, site entry, and quality of collateral materials were also equal or better (Presentation). It did not appear that these elements needed adjusting.

Even though the suggested changes reduced our margins significantly and dropped our financial return, we chose to try them out and gave the team the green light to go forward. Over the next four months the changes were made.

Four months later, we had new, smaller products at lower prices and had a competitive closing incentive package that the salesperson had designed. However, the sales performance was still substandard compared to the competition.

At this point, we asked the team what they recommended and the answer was more price reductions.

However, when compared to the competitors, our absolute pricing level and price per square foot were already lower, and our new floor plans were actually better. As a senior management team, we then looked and said that the only P we had not tinkered with was the People P. We had to do it, or at least try, even though the salesperson had done well and had been with us for nearly a decade.

So, in the final "test," we moved the salesperson to another community and took that community's sales manager, who had less seniority and experience, and moved him to Buckingham.

Within a month, magically the sales rate picked up in the Buckingham community, and within two months the pace was fast enough that we could actually reduce the incentive and raise prices.

We came to believe that the sales skills of the original person worked fine in a good market. But the discipline needed to sell in a soft market just wasn't there. In a subsequent review, her performance at the "new" community was also weak. Sales were less than the level attained by the salesperson that we had transferred to Buckingham. Within a couple of months of the test, it was apparent to both of us that it wasn't going to work in this new environment, and we parted ways.

In retrospect, using the 7 P's and focusing on all but the People P allowed a structured experiment to occur to adapt to the marketplace. If the non-people adjustments did not work, the only variable left to try was changing people.

Our organization took the process as a fair and equitable one, and it actually boosted morale in a difficult time. Teams had input, a structure to present that input, and a way to look at performance in an organized way. The seven P's had proven their worth.

## *"The 7 P's: Product, Price, Place, Promotion, People, Process, and Presentation."*

Exercise: Take two competing products, services, or businesses and analyze them using the 7 P's. What do you learn? What would you change for each in order to make them more competitive?

_____

_____

_____

_____

_____

_____

_____

_____

_____

_____

_____

_____

_____

_____

_____

_____

# 28

## THE BALANCING ACT

*The task of the senior executive is to balance management of both the income statement and the balance sheet. This measurement, return on assets, can be influenced through knowledge of the DuPont formula. Of the initiatives that an executive can undertake using the DuPont formula, working on improvement of cycle time is the hardest, yet most in the control of the company. It is oftentimes the most rewarding.*

Learning the skills of general management can be daunting. Sooner or later one has to understand the fundamental operations of the enterprise (what your product is, how you produce it and the business model that leads to profitability), how the enterprise fits into a competitive and regulatory environment, how the enterprise finances itself, and how to balance the interests of stakeholders (customers, employees, investors, and the broader community).

In learning these skills, it sometimes becomes easy to forget that business enterprises are formed to serve the needs of customers. By doing this well, the business hopefully generates value in excess of cost (the profit). The final step is that the profit has to be sufficient to satisfy the needs of the capital invested in the company.

The executive has a fundamental responsibility to manage both the income statement (the operations of the enterprise and its profitability) and the balance sheet (how much money the enterprise has invested in it) and where that capital is deployed. The friction between the two is risk.

In order to create a profit, the enterprise takes on various risks: will the product have market acceptance, will there be sufficient value to create a profit, will that profit be sufficient to satisfy the capital invested in the business, compared to other uses the capital could entertain. If the enterprise creates returns that are better than alternate investments that capital could make for the same level of risk, the business most likely retains its capital or can attract more. If it does not, the enterprise will ultimately wither and die.

When I took my basic finance courses, we were jammed full of financial analysis tools in a short period of time. The more I progressed in my general management learning, the more I came to appreciate one tool, the DuPont formula, as highly important in being able to bring simplicity and clarity to often complex business evaluations.

Forgetting the lessons of the formula condemns a manager to being caught up in the trivia of the enterprise and missing out on the important trends and factors that lead to understandings about both the underlying health of the business and the levels of risk that the company is undertaking.

The DuPont formula, or model as it is sometimes called, is credited to F. Donaldson Brown, who joined the treasury department of the DuPont Powder Company in 1914. Seeking a tool that integrated elements of both the income statement and the balance sheet, Brown devised the model.

Later, DuPont purchased 23 percent of General Motors Corporation, which was in financial difficulty at the time, and Brown was given the job of helping to clean up the company's finances under the direction of the legendary Alfred Sloan. Brown used the system to help develop a set of planning and control systems that are credited with helping to turn the company around.

The system then migrated to a variety of companies and became the basis of best practice in a variety of companies for years.

The ideas for the DuPont model are simple:

- The core measurement that integrates the income statement and the balance sheet is return on assets (ROA). This measures pretax profit against the total assets invested in the business. This measurement is done before any cost of debt is considered. The simple idea is that if the return on assets is greater than the cost of capital, then looking at that source of capital as appropriate for the business is warranted. For example, if a company only has a 3 percent return on assets, putting debt that costs 6 percent on the enterprise is a sure-fire way to dilute the value of the equity in the business. On the other hand, if the ROA is, say, 30 percent, at least considering capital sources that have costs less than 30 percent is warranted. Then, the risks of that capital in the business can be evaluated.

- Return on assets is really composed of two key pieces: the pre-interest profitability that you have on sales, measured as a percentage, and sales revenues for the year, compared to the assets of the company. The pre-interest profitability is expressed in accounting jargon as EBIDTA (Earnings before Interest, Depreciation, Taxes, and Amortization.) If you have a business that has a 5 percent EBIDTA and your annual sales revenues are three times the capital you have invested, the annual return on assets is 15 percent (5 percent times the three times that the capital turns in the year).

- There are subcomponents of the model that can be tracked and managed in order to try to improve the overall return.

In Appendix I, there is a more complete explanation of the DuPont formula, its components, and how those components interrelate in the effort to improve return on assets.

To summarize Appendix I, there are three key areas of the DuPont formula: *creating value* (expressed in the two metrics. gross profit/sales and sales/cost of goods sold, or COGS), *watching your overhead* (expressed as the ratio EBIDTA/gross profit), and *improving capital turns* by both watching dead inventory and focusing on production cycle time (all expressed in the ratio COGS/assets).

By working on all of these items, the return on the assets invested in a business should get better.

I had the opportunity in the late 1990s and early 2000s to work on this issue at the Weston master planned community in South Florida for Arvida.

Arvida was not only the developer of the community, but also did the majority of the homebuilding.

Arriving in mid-1998, I had an assignment to substantially complete the community by September of 2002. The primary task involved the sale of approximately five thousand homes and the construction and closing of nearly six thousand in a period of almost five years. (Attendant to this was the manufacture of over three thousand building lots, the creation of another $10 million in amenities, the creation and sale of the "downtown" of the community, and the sale of all other assets we had in the community also.)

Although the community had been selling in excess of one thousand homes per year, it was stuck at a production rate that hovered in the 850-900 homes per year range. It was pretty obvious that keeping at those levels was not going to get us out in time.

The market for available subcontractors was tough. All builders had more work than the trade base could handle, and any new additions typically had bad quality and were expensive. So just throwing more manpower at the problem was not a reasonable solution, either.

What did catch my eye was the fact that little tracking of the cycle time of production had been done. When we did start to do it, it appeared that our smaller homes seemed to take between 180 and 250 days to complete and our larger homes took from 330 to over 400 days. These were normal production times in the marketplace.

I had come from an experience where, by working on process improvement and cycle time reduction, we had produced similar sized homes in the 80-120 day range.

A review of the home construction operation showed that the most common occurrence any day in a house was that nothing was being done. In financial terms, the assets were laying fallow most of the time and not getting any closer to the time when the capital could be re-harvested and put back to work again. In 1997, the return on assets for the community was 16.3 percent (doing slightly over eight hundred homes with a sales value of $148 million, which created $19.6 million of EBIDTA on a $120 million asset base).

So the problem was how to step up both production and sales to a point that we could liquidate the assets in time to meet our legal obligations and to make as much money as possible while doing so. Of course, we had to work at keeping our customer satisfaction up (deterioration would mean slower sales and/or less margin on sales) and our investors wanted a higher return on their invested capital, too.

To address the problem took a multipronged approach that was influenced by thinking about DuPont.

The operation was performing beyond its breakeven point and a reasonable percentage of the gross profit (between 50 percent and 60 percent) was flowing to EBIDTA. Overhead eating up all the gross profit was not a major concern.

By increasing the throughput (number of homes delivered per year) at a rate faster than growing the overhead needed to ramp up production, our EBIDTA/gross profit ratio would get even better and more dollars would flow to the bottom line as we extended further and further past our breakeven point. To do this, though, we had to make sure that we kept our fixed costs tightly controlled. To grow production, we knew that the absolute dollars spent on overhead had to grow. The question was whether the volume effect of the growth would actually drive the percentage of overhead to gross profit down.

In 1997, the overall gross margin was 22 percent. This was low for a builder developer. In part, it reflected an issue with costs of production and, in part, it reflected a mix issue.

The costs of production had been rising quickly in the Florida market, as there was more demand for trade labor and supplies than there was available supply. Unfortunately, because houses were sold long before they could be built and took a long time to build, the costs of building were escalating in a time when the selling price of the house had been fixed by the fact that it was already under contract.

A further review showed that the smaller homes, which were built somewhat faster than the larger homes and were easier to sell, had lower margins at the time of sale than the larger ones and were proportionately more of the closings.

To solve this, we had several opportunities. The first was to try to build homes more quickly, thereby trying to cut back the amount of profit margin erosion that happened between the time of sale and closing due to long delivery times. The second was to test pushing up pricing to try to get some compensation for the long-term option at a fixed price that customers were enjoying. The final idea was to try to add more profit by having a better program for offering pre-priced options for the homes.

When we looked at the options that people were putting in the homes, the ratio, particularly in the mid-and high-priced homes, was around 6 percent to

7 percent of the base selling price. An industry norm was around 10 percent for mid-priced homes and near 15 percent for high-priced homes. If we could do this without slowing down production times, we could get more profit out of each home and increase our gross margin.

Finally, the cycle time of production had to be addressed. The ratio of cost of goods sold to assets, indicating how quickly the assets were being turned, stood at .95. This was indicative mostly of the long times it took to build houses and the fact that the capital just sat out there. If we could try to cut our house construction times in half, mostly just by tight scheduling to ensure that work was going on every day, then we had the chance to double our ratio.

It took until early 1999 to put an organization in place to do these things (see "Organizations tend to do the things they are organized to do"), including a central function for process control and improvement that focused on an even flow of production, cycle time reduction, and quality improvement. By the year 2000, the operation was in full swing and we were delivering north of twelve hundred homes per year, cycle times were falling dramatically, and our efforts on margin improvement were beginning to show.

By the end of 2001, the return on assets had climbed from 16.3 percent in 1997 to 102.7 percent. In 2001, nearly fifteen hundred homes were closed, and we knew that we would be able to meet the end of September 2002 deadline to have our operations fundamentally wound up.

Each of the factors we had worked on had an impact. Controlling the fixed overhead and driving more volume though our fixed overhead took us far past our breakeven point. Our EBIDTA/gross profit (how much of our gross profit made it to the bottom line) increased from 60 percent to 77 percent.

Our Focus on cycle time improvement, cutting the time from sale to closing, plus working on pushing up pricing and adding more options, allowed our gross margin to improve from 22 percent to 37 percent.

But, most important, the focus on cycle time improvement (we ultimately got the small houses built in ninety days and the largest in 135 days), allowed the asset turns (Cost of Goods Sold to Assets) to improve from .95 to 2.31.

Without a doubt, the focus on cycle time improvement had the largest bang for the buck. Not only did it improve our capital turns, but it also allowed us to stem some of the margin deterioration that occurred, just because costs kept rising in a hot market.

However, the focus in the other areas bore fruit also. Although not as dramatic as the cycle time improvement, by the time they all leveraged off of each other, the compounding effect of all factors working together was dramatic.

If the improvement had only come in the number of homes delivered per year and the margin and cycle times had remained constant to 1997, the return on assets would have improved from 16.3 percent in 1997 to 20.9 percent in 2001. Driving higher throughput has an impact, but the return on assets only would have improved by 28 percent over the four year period.

If margin had been the only thing to change and throughput and cycle time remained constant, the return on assets would have improved from 16.3 percent in 1997 to 32.9 percent in 2001, or an improvement of 102 percent. That was much more powerful.

Clearly, improvement of margin had a bigger impact than just improving throughput. However, we must remember that some of this margin improvement was due to the shorter cycle times forestalling some of the margin deterioration.

Finally, if throughput and margin had stayed the same and only the cycle time improvements had occurred, the return on assets would have improved from 16.3 percent in 1997 to 39.6 percent in 2001. This would have been a 143 percent improvement over four years. Although more powerful than the other two factors individually, it still is not an eye-popper.

It is when all of the factors start to work together that dramatic improvements in the financial returns occur. When all of the factors are improving at the same time, the effects compound on one another.

However, increasing throughput is somewhat limited by the size of the market you are in and the market share you can garner. Increasing margin is limited by your market power and the competitive landscape.

Improving cycle time is nearly totally in your hands. It is hard, takes organization, technology, and creativity and involves the greatest amount of internal change. But, if accomplished, it most often has the greatest impact. And that is the lesson.

## *"Improving cycle time is almost always a good thing to do."*

Exercise: Take your company (or a public company with good available financial information) and determine the return on assets for the past three years using the DuPont model. What do you learn? What is getting better, and what is getting worse? If you could improve the cycle time of your most important value generation process by 50 percent, what impact would it have on the return on assets?

_____

_____

_____

_____

_____

_____

_____

_____

_____

_____

_____

_____

_____

_____

# 29

## GOING WITH THE FLOW

*Adopting a strategy of even flow of work enables volume variance to be eliminated and allows focus to be placed on the reduction of process variances. This strategy can lead to faster cycle times, fewer defects, and higher profitability, even if the even flow is later removed or modified.*

I learned the homebuilding business from the ground up. You sold a house, built it, and then closed it. If you sold two houses at the same time, you tried to build them simultaneously. If you sold more houses, you tried to build them, too, all at the same time. It usually took longer, but, heck, that was homebuilding. Sooner or later you sold more houses than you could start, and you developed a backlog of sales that had not started yet, but you tried to start them as quickly as you could.

The business was always in flux. You tended to sell more houses in the spring because people wanted to move into their new house over the summer so that their kids could be in the new school when the school year started. Building in the Middle Atlantic States (Pennsylvania and New Jersey) also meant that weather had to be taken into consideration. There was a push to start houses before the frost hit and to get them "dried in" before winter really hit, so that crews could work inside during the winter months.

When Toll Brothers, my first employer in home-building, went public in the mid-1980s, we had the additional constraint of trying to get closings in to meet a quarter or year-end target and satisfy our representations to the analysts on Wall Street. The end result was a very "bumpy" flow in production; no starts for three weeks, then eight; or no closings for three weeks and then trying to get twenty in the last month of the quarter.

The time it took to build a house varied widely. Customers called regularly to wonder why no work was going on in their house. The rush to get large volumes of houses done at the same time led to quality issues. Work was left incomplete or was just done wrong. This led to long lists for the warranty department after the house closed and inevitable customer dissatisfaction. It was the way the industry ran.

In the early 1990s, I met the owners who ran Wayne Homes in North Canton, Ohio, and, soon after, the partners at RayCo (the old Ray Ellison Homes in San Antonio, Texas). I was on a personal search to try to figure out what organizational structure gave the best financial results: a project management structure or a functional-based structure. Both of these companies came to my attention because they had financial returns that were significantly better than the rest of the industry. Both had unleveraged returns on assets in the 35 percent to 40 percent range and returns on equity in the 75 percent plus range. These were double to triple the norms in the industry.

I wanted to see if the way they were organized was the reason they were so much better.

I first met with Wayne Homes and, in the initial discussion, asked the normal question, "How many homes a year do you do?" The company's response was interesting: "Six hundred. We do twelve a week for fifty weeks and then take two weeks off for Christmas and New Year's." It was late spring, and the company further noted: "we have sold out of our production for the year." These were new concepts for me: a fixed number of homes per week and an absolute limitation on the number of homes delivered per year. I asked whether, if the market was hot, they would add in a couple of extra closings for the year to try to make more money for the year and got just a quizzical look for my efforts and a succinct "no."

I then went to RayCo. I remember going into the office of Jack Robinson, the chief operating officer at the time. His desk was clean except for a single sheet of paper. I asked Jack how many homes he did per year and his response was: "Well, it is around twenty-four hundred, but it is really ten a day, every day." (By the way, that was about 50 percent of the San Antonio market.) The sheet on his desk listed the key elements of the building operations for the previous day: permits received, footings dug, slabs poured, frames started, frames finished, drywall completed, pre-closing walk-throughs with customers, etc. Next to it was the number of homes that had completed that stage of construction for the previous day, and the goal was ten.

If it was a number different than ten, there was a discussion with his managers the first thing in the morning, and they were on to corrective action by 8 a.m.

He allowed that sales were never even, but that they sold into "slots," so the customer knew when his or her "slot" would start and finish. If the sales pace was too fast and the slots moved too far out, the company withheld product from the market or raised prices. If it was too slow, the company reduced prices or considered dropping the pace from ten to a lower number (that rarely happened).

Since Jack had worked as a supervisor at a Frito Lay potato chip plant near Dallas, I could see how the logic was derived. It was like he had a conveyor belt and the factory was set to produce a certain number of bags of chips per hour, only in this case it was houses moving down RayCo's conveyor belt.

What was interesting was that the folks at Wayne and RayCo had never met one another. Yet they both had come upon a technique called even flow, and the financial results were strikingly similar for both companies. Not only from a financial standpoint were they similar, but they both had very fast cycle times for building homes, very high ratios of homes delivered per employee, and very low defect rates (and correspondingly low warranty expenses as a percentage of sales).

It was the embodiment of systems and structures determine outcomes (the Beer Game). They operated differently than all of the other homebuilders, and their results were remarkably better because of that difference.

Both were also organized on a functional basis (a head of construction, a head of sales, a head of marketing, etc.) rather than a project management basis. But most of the industry was organized that way also.

The apparent differentiator was that these companies had a daily target and a weekly target of production pace (twelve per week for Wayne and ten per day for RayCo), and they could easily measure themselves against those targets. This was "management by the day, get results by the day" in full operation.

They had full "closed-loop" meetings with all of the functional heads involved in production to ensure that houses were started on schedule and remained on schedule. The person who ran the operation at RayCo was a woman with an accounting background. Not the typical head of operations in a homebuilding company.

As I dug into the rationale behind this much-different way of operating from the rest of the industry, I also began to take some courses in Total Quality Management. What began to dawn on me was that, if you wanted to improve the performance of a process or an organization, it was easier to do if the volume or throughput was a constant, since there were really two root causes of deviation: process variance and volume variance. If you could eliminate volume variance by adopting an even flow, the only thing left to work on was process variance. You could then, as a management team, focus on improving those processes, which usually led to faster cycle times, lower defect rates, and more efficient ways of doing things.

All of these factors have a positive impact on the financial returns of a company as well as on the mental health of the employees. Rather than feeling like "Lucy on the candy line" (where Lucille Ball and Ethel Mertz in the TV show "I Love Lucy" were trying to eat the chocolates because they could not wrap them fast enough), employees in a stable volume environment feel more in control of their work, and managers can figure out how to correctly staff to do the work and where there are process problems and opportunities for improvement.

It is no surprise that this logic played a role in the work we did several years later at Weston, described in the DuPont chapter. By setting a pace of five per day (twenty-five per week), we knew that we were on a pace to do 1,250 homes per year and that would have us completed in time, four years hence. The standardization of the flow allowed us to do the process improvement pieces that both enabled better financial returns and also gave a higher predictability to what we were doing. That predictability enabled us to better set customer expectations and led to higher customer satisfaction (95 percent highly willing to refer at the end). The higher satisfaction, in turn, helped to drive sales. It was truly a win-win.

Getting an even flow of production was not an easy task. We had to establish a Process Control and Improvement group, and it was its job to get us onto an even flow and to then improve processes that helped to reduce our cycle time, reduce our defect rates and warranty, and improve our customer satisfaction. The key tools for making this transition were a closed-loop meeting, a visual calendar with a magnetic tag for each home in production, and a set of charts that displayed how we were doing over time (starts per day, cycle time for major phases of construction, customer satisfaction scores, etc.).

It was a combination of two ideas: organizations tending to do the things they are organized to do, and a change to the systems and structures of the business in order to get a different result.

Everyone involved with the starting of the home, both inside of the company plus key trade partners, met once a week to plan the starts on a day-by-day basis for the upcoming six weeks. Then, several times during the week, subgroups would meet at the magnetic calendar boards to review how they were doing. All was measured against the standard of five per day and twenty-five per week.

The permitting staff would review how it was doing at obtaining building permits and all other paperwork in order to start the home. The construction managers would review how houses were doing against their schedule on a daily basis and act on problem areas. The staff charged with closing the home with the customer reviewed that process with representatives of the mortgage lenders and the title and escrow agents.

The goal was to manage problems on a very frequent basis and to begin to learn where there were persistent problems so that they could be eliminated permanently. Piece by piece things got better, and people got comfortable with having tighter control on events.

For example, one of the persistent defects early on was waiting for plans from our architect to submit with the building permit application to the Broward County building official. We found that, even though the representative from the architect was at our weekly planning meeting, he was not relaying the planned schedule to his internal managers. Our process improvement team had to go to the architect's office and set up an internal system for the staff to follow and then run the system for a while until the managers were trained and became comfortable with managing to the master plan developed each week. In the process, the architect became more efficient, and a defect had been put to bed.

This is a business model that, I subsequently learned, was utilized by DiVosta Homes in West Palm Beach, Florida (now a division of Pulte Homes), with similar results. As we noted in the "Beer" chapter, systems and structures determine outcomes. Even-flow techniques create a system and structure that can help make an organization more productive and profitable.

As an adjunct to this method of interactive planning, I am often confronted with the complaint that even flow is hard to do in up and down markets. My response is that even flow does not have to last forever.

A company may be able to run a pace of, say, three per week for four months and then drop to two per week for six months and then increase back to three per week. The key is that all of the participants in the production cycle have to agree that they can correctly staff for that pace and agree to abide by it.

I also remind managers that even flow is most important as a way for improving processes both internally and among your suppliers. Once processes have been improved and those improvements are embedded, even uneven flow works better than before, but it never will work as good as the even flow. When everyone understands what the daily or weekly plan is, somehow it works out better for everyone.

*"An even flow of work leads to faster cycle times, fewer defects, and higher profitability."*

Exercise: Does your business attempt to work on an even flow of work? Does it help? If not, what would be the impediments to doing it? Do you think it would help?

---

---

---

---

---

---

---

---

---

---

---

---

---

---

---

---

---

---

---

---

---

# 30

## IS THE JUICE WORTH THE
## SQUEEZE?

*The habit of learning from successes and failures and then passing that wisdom on to others in the organization is the key to long-term organizational growth and success. Do you extract the juice of wisdom from the fruits of experience every day?*

As much as the business schools would like to believe that management is a science, many managers would contend that it is really a mixture of science, experience, and art form.

In science, one performs experiments and, from those experiments, comes to conclusions and theories about how things work so that they can be predicted with certainty into the future. The theories are a form of experience that can be called upon in order to know what will probably happen when the same factors or ingredients are brought together again in the future. That knowledge can be transmitted to others so that they may benefit from the experience, also.

In doing so, the chances of handling challenges successfully in the future are raised.

Since business and management add the factor of people to the experiment, and people are different, theories of management and business have a wild-card factor that physics, chemistry, biology, mathematics, and other pure sciences do not have. It does not mean that generalizations about business and management cannot be made and lessons cannot be learned from the experiences of others. It does mean that they are not as pure as the theories from the "hard" sciences and have to be given some skepticism when applied.

Oscar Wilde is sometimes credited with the observation that "Experience is the name everyone gives to their mistakes." Bob Pachwood takes it further: "Judgment comes from experience, and great judgment comes from bad experience." G. Warren Nutter adds his twist: "Good judgment comes from experience. Experience comes from bad judgment." And, finally, Confucius throws in his two-cents' worth: "There are three methods of gaining wisdom. The first is reflection, which is the highest. The second is imitation, which is the easiest. The third is experience, which is the bitterest."

This circular relationship between wisdom, experience, and judgment is an important one to understand. As I noted early: "It is a wise man who knows that which he does not know." If we are to be good, effective managers and leaders, we have to understand that reflection, imitation, and experience are the potential sources of the wisdom needed for the judgments we must make.

We also must understand that sometimes we will get it wrong and that "experience," if understood and reflected upon, will hopefully lead to better wisdom and judgments in the future.

This book has been written to perhaps provide some of the wisdom, experience, and lessons that I have acquired, so that others can utilize them in the formation of their own wisdom by taking and learning from the experiences I have observed and analyzed and tried to distill into the simple snippets of knowledge presented.

The most important lesson, however, I probably derived from the "Beer" chapter, where we learned that systems and structures primarily determine outcomes. If a manager knows what has to be done and then organizes to do it, the probability of success is improved.

To improve that probability even further, one needs to make sure that the organization itself can learn from its experiences and then adapt to those lessons. It is a good habit for an organization to develop.

If managers ask themselves and the people who report to them the question "What did I learn today" or "What did I learn from that experience," the underpinnings for gaining knowledge, from both good and bad judgments and good and bad experiences, will be in place.

The basis for improvement comes from such learning.

To be effective, the process has to be without fear or arrogance. A manager and his charges have to understand that errors will be made, and that one has to learn from those errors in order to not make them again. They have to also understand that victories, even if celebrated, can easily become defeats the next time if lessons are not learned from them, too.

I am continually impressed by the great coaches and athletes who, even walking away from a victory, note the things that did not work well and have to be worked on in the coming week. They are humble and understand that the next victory is never assured unless there is an ethic of improvement. I admire athletes such as the quarterbacks Tom Brady and Peyton Manning. Even in victory, they are finding things that need to be worked on, and they then work on them in the following week.

If a manager creates an environment of critical review and learning, the people will grow and the organization will do well in the long term. If there is fear, political recrimination, or other impediments to the process of open learning and application of that learning, I can almost guarantee that the organization will not do well over time.

Early in the book, I reviewed the lesson embodied in the phrase "Is the juice worth the squeeze?" As this book ends, I hope that managers can see that there is a second lesson in this phrase that is linked to gaining wisdom. The fruits (sometimes bitter and sometimes sweet) of personal and organizational experiences have to be distilled into the juices of wisdom that can be passed on to others.

Managers who develop the habit of asking people "What did you learn today" and then taking that learning and condensing it into stories, phrases, and other memorable mnemonics and aphorisms have a leg up on their competition for a very long time.

*"The habit of extracting the juices of wisdom from the fruits of experience is a good one to learn and teach to others."*

Exercise: How is wisdom currently passed on in your organization? Does it work?

_____

_____

_____

_____

_____

_____

_____

_____

_____

_____

_____

_____

_____

_____

_____

_____

_____

_____

_____

_____

# Epilogue

The habit of extracting wisdom from experience applies both inside of business and in everyday life. The experiences that can be evaluated can be personal and they can be via observation. The important trait is to slow down, think about things, and then see if there is a lesson that can be learned.

I started writing this book in the summer of 2009 as the country was in the middle of the Great Recession. The government was trying to craft policy responses to both the Great Recession and to some of the agenda that President Barack Obama brought to Washington with his election the prior year.

During this period, many books were written about the events, particularly on Wall Street, which either caused the financial collapse or were impacted by them. History was being either made or was being newly analyzed on nearly a daily basis.

As I began to think about what I had seen and experienced, I started to extract a couple more cups of juice from what I had seen or was seeing.

The first one was that if the government was throwing money out the window; figure out how to stand in the way. It was becoming pretty obvious that, for a while, policy was favoring health care, "green" initiatives, and centralization of power in Washington, D.C. Companies which had some involvement with health care, even tangential, would probably do pretty well. Biotech research, medical office buildings, software that made medical recordkeeping easier, and similar efforts would probably be pretty good places to be, for example.

Similarly, companies involved with alternative energy, resource conservation, and the education of these things were going to do pretty well for a while.

It was no surprise that my friends in real estate in the Washington, D.C., area were coming out of the slump faster than most. Somehow federal government spending tends to stay close to home. A new item had the counties surrounding Washington as some of the most affluent in the country.

The second observation really was one tied to the financial collapse. It seemed to me the lesson was: "Beware apparent truths that are easily financed."

For many decades, some of the "accepted truths" of our society were the following:

- Owning your own home is the American dream.
- To get ahead you have to go to college.
- You have to trade your car every three years.

Each of these was enabled by either policy incentives from Washington or easily available financing, or both. The financing for houses became so easy that a strawberry picker in California earning $14,000 per year could buy a $750,000 home (of course, he never made any payments on the mortgage). College financing became easy to get and students graduated with huge debts, but with skills that did not provide the ability to earn anywhere near the income required to pay off the debt.

Huge government subsidy and guaranty programs (Fannie Mae, Sallie Mae, and Freddie Mac) essentially transferred the risk of nonpayment over to the government. Bankers and intermediaries won; ordinary citizens sometimes won and often lost.

As we now have to pay the piper and look at socialized debts plus government borrowing increases, the lessons have to be remembered. It will be hard enough handling the detritus of the past excess. Trying to escape new schemes will be important.

Finally, I think that I have learned that leadership matters. The companies and organizations that have made it through have mostly had great leaders. Those who have suffered and failed mostly did not. So picking your leaders is ever more important, whether it is in the choosing of what company you work for (make evaluation of the leader something that is important to you), what government leaders we elect, or what management teams we approve as investors.

I truly hope that each of you develops that habit of extracting wisdom every day, and passes the lessons and the skill on to your workmates, employees, and, most of all, your kids.

# Appendix I

## THE DUPONT FORMULA

*The DuPont formula is important for managers to know. It provides a framework for improvement of a company's return on assets: the key measurement of the balance between income statement management and balance sheet management.*

The DuPont formula, or model as it is sometimes called, is credited to F. Donaldson Brown, who joined the treasury department of the DuPont Powder Company in 1914. Seeking a tool that integrated elements of both the income statement and the balance sheet, Brown devised the model.

Later, DuPont purchased 23 percent of General Motors Corporation, which was having financial difficulties, and Brown was given the job of helping to clean up the company's finances under the direction of the legendary Alfred Sloan. Brown used the system to help develop a set of planning and control systems that are credited with helping to turn the company around. The system then migrated to a variety of companies and became the basis of best practice in companies for years.

The ideas for the DuPont model are simple:

- The core measurement that integrates the income statement and the balance sheet is return on assets (ROA), which measures pretax profit against the total assets invested in the business. This measurement is done before any cost of debt (leverage) is put on the enterprise. The simple idea is that if the profit (EBIDTA: Earnings before Interest, Depreciation, Taxes, and Amortization) divided by the total assets of the company (which is also equal to the totality of liabilities and equity, by definition) is greater than a cost of capital (debt, preferred stock, etc.), then looking at that source of capital as appropriate for the business is warranted. If a company only has a 3 percent return on assets, putting 6 percent debt on the enterprise is a sure-fire way to dilute the value of the equity in the business. On the other hand, if the unleveraged return is, say, 30 percent, at least considering capital sources that have costs less than 30% is warranted and, then, the risks of that capital in the business can be evaluated.

- Return on assets is really composed of two key pieces: the profitability that you have on a sale and how many of those sales can you do in a year, compared to the assets (the same as capital) that are invested in the company. If you have a business that has a 5 percent profit on sales and your annual sales amount is three times the capital you have invested, the annual return on assets is 15 percent (5 percent times the three times that the capital turns in the year).

- There are subcomponents of the model that can be tracked and managed in order to try to improve the overall return.

I had read and thought that I understood the formula, but had trouble taking the concept and trying to practically apply it to managing an enterprise on a day to day basis. Finally, using some basic algebra one day, I was able to make sense of the formula and put it into a set of concepts that I could both manage to and teach to my managers.

First, I had to break apart the income statement:

|  | |
|---|---|
| | **SALES** |
| — | **COGS (COST OF GOODS SOLD)** |
| = | **GP (GROSS PROFIT)** |
| — | **OH (all overhead items)** |
| = | **EBIDTA** |
| | (Earnings before Interest, Depreciation, Taxes, and Amortization) |

**SALES** are all of the revenues that the company gets from the sale of its products to others.

**COST OF GOODS SOLD** is the direct costs used to create the product that is being sold. In the home-building business, this consists of the improved lot you build upon plus the bricks and sticks cost of the home itself. For most businesses, this consists of the labor and materials, both incurred in the company and contracted out to others, to create the product or services that are being conveyed to customers.

**GROSS PROFIT** is what is left over from the sales revenues after paying for the direct costs of what was sold. This is a measure of the value that is created. If you can sell something for more than its inherent cost, you have created value. That value then has to pay for the **Overhead** (selling costs, marketing, general and administrative expenses) that was needed to support the creation and sales of the product.

Anything left over from that is profit, which is expressed as **EBIDTA**, or Earnings before Interest, Depreciation, Taxes, and Amortization. By using this measure, the distorting effects of leverage (debt) are factored out of the analysis, permitting the ratio of **EBIDTA/ASSETS** to be compared to the various costs of different kinds of capital.

The basic DuPont formula is unchanged from its inception:

$$\frac{EBIDTA}{ASSETS} = \frac{EBIDTA}{SALES} \times \frac{SALES}{ASSETS}$$

In this analysis, here is what the pieces mean:
**EBIDTA/ASSETS** (or return on assets [ROA]) is the measure of the return on the capital invested in the business (since capital, by definition, equals the assets of a company). Without debt, capital is also equal to the equity in the business. Think of this as the equivalent of the earnings you get on a savings account at a bank. If you have $100 in a bank account and the bank pays you $5 interest for a year, the yield or return on that $100 is 5 percent (5/100). In a company, the same idea holds. If you invest $100 in the company and that $100 is invested in inventory, machines, plant, copiers,

etc. and you earn $5 in profit, you have a 5 percent return on that invested capital (which is the same as a 5 percent return on assets).

When the algebra is applied, **EBIDTA/ASSETS** consists of two factors multiplied by each other.

**EBIDTA/SALES** represents the profit that is made on the sales the company makes. When a company says that it makes a 10 percent pretax profit margin, it means that after the costs of production (cost of goods sold) and overhead are deducted from the sales revenues, what is left is profit. In order to take out the factors of interest, depreciation, the write-off (amortization) of good will and other intangible assets and taxes, the formula focuses on the profit (or earnings) before these factors to get a clear look at the company's finances.

**SALES/ASSETS** represents how large the sales of the company are compared to the capital or assets invested in the company and used to create the platform for those sales. This is sometimes called capital turns or capital productivity. I think of it in terms of a waitress working at a diner and making tips from the service of a single table. If the average tip is $3 on a $15 dinner check (big tippers paying a 20 percent tip) and she just has one set of customers in her shift, she makes a 20 percent return on that table. However, if she can get three sets of customers to use the table during a shift, she can make $9 instead of $3 against that table. It is why restaurants try to turn their tables multiple times an evening. The wait staff and the owner make more money from the same asset base (the kitchen and the tables).

If we think of this in terms of the DuPont formula, the waitress makes an **EBIDTA/SALES** of 20 percent on her three turns of the table for the evening ($9 in tips on $45 in check revenues for the evening). If the table was worth, say, $90 (and further assume that the owner made her buy her own table), her sales/assets would be 50 percent ($45 in sales compared to the $90 table). Multiplying the two together (20 percent x 50 percent), she would have a 10 percent return on that table for the evening, or a 3,650 percent return on the table for the year.

Although this is a simplistic example, the idea is the same. If she had two tables and could handle both of them, her return would still be the same, however, her actual cash income would be double. Twice the investment, twice the cash income.

I had known about the DuPont formula for about twenty years, but had a hard time applying it to the management of a business. Having a higher profit margin was better than having a lower profit margin. I got that part.

However, the asset turn piece **(SALES/ASSETS)** confounded me. What were the things I could do and measure that made that ratio get better?

Mathematics is the language of engineering and one day I started to play with the formula just to see how the formula pieces could be broken down further into other pieces, which, when multiplied by each other, still gave the final answer of **EBIDTA/ASSETS**, just as the DuPont formula always did.

I was looking for metrics that I understood as part of the normal management of the business so that I could figure out how to then take concrete management actions that would improve the metrics that drove getting the return on assets of the enterprise to improve.

The first piece that I attacked was core profitability: **EBIDTA/SALES.** This could be broken, in turn, into two pieces, which, when multiplied by each other gave **EBIDTA/SALES.** The pieces turned out this way:

$$\frac{\textbf{EBIDTA}}{\textbf{SALES}} = \frac{\textbf{EBIDTA}}{\textbf{GROSS PROFIT}} \times \frac{\textbf{GROSS PROFIT}}{\textbf{SALES}}$$

In the case of the first factor, **EBIDTA/GROSS PROFIT**, this represented **overhead efficiency**: how much of the gross profit got eaten up in the overhead of the company and, thusly, how much was left for profit.

The core idea here is that people pay for value created, not the "overhead friction" that doesn't add value.

For example, the customer doesn't really care whether your office is on the good side of town or the bad side if they are buying the product at a department store. Whether your rent is $100 per month or $10,000 per month is irrelevant to the customer. Yet this is a piece of the "friction" of overhead that stands between the gross profit and the core profitability metric of EBIDTA.

If all of the gross profit is eaten up in overhead, EBIDTA becomes zero and, no matter how much value was created in the product, the return on assets will be zero. The goal here is to get the **EBIDTA/GROSS PROFIT** ratio as high as possible.

Tracking it with time gives a sense of how well those efforts are proceeding. In the trauma of the Great

Recession, understanding the erosion of profit that is due to excess overhead has become intense. The costs of employee benefits, location costs, and other overhead items have come under intense scrutiny as gross profits have been squeezed in an ever-competitive market. Companies are learning that once overhead is added, it is very difficult to reduce.

The lesson is that care and thought in adding overhead that is not easily variable with market conditions has to be evaluated critically.

Volume has an impact on **EBIDTA/GROSS PROFIT**. To the extent more activity can be run through a fixed overhead, efficiency is improved and EBIDTA grows. For example, a business might need a controller/bookkeeper even at a low level of business, say sales of $250,000 per year. That controller/bookkeeper might be able to handle a business level up to $2 million per year before needing help. If the bookkeeper cost $50,000 per year, that represents 20 percent of sales at the lower volume and 2.5 percent of sales at the higher volume. To the extent that overhead is truly fixed, adding volume tends to help spreading that fixed overhead over more sales and the proportion of gross profit that is eaten up by overhead correspondingly reduces. That is all good for this first metric.

The second factor, **GROSS PROFIT/SALES**, is often called gross margin and is frequently expressed as a percentage of the selling price: for example, we have a 50 percent gross margin. In its simplest understanding, this is a measure of the value created by the company and appreciated by its customers to the point that they are willing to pay more for the product than the intrinsic costs it takes to make the product.

Value is influenced by many factors, both tangible and intangible. In the chapter on the 7 P's, we saw how intangible factors such as design innovation, service delivery, quality of sales force, location of sale, etc. could influence the price that a customer is willing to pay for a product.

Similarly, the operational items, such as ability to negotiate lower prices for direct costs of materials and labor or reducing the costs of defects and rework, impact the gross profit significantly also. Together they create the ability to generate value that is in excess of cost and this is the core measure of the viability of a business, since it reflects value created in the eyes of the customer.

So, in summary, the first piece of the DuPont formula (**EBIDTA/SALES**, or profitability) can be thought of in two pieces: how much value is created and, then, how much of that value makes it to the bottom line. By focusing on the things that make higher value and the things and decisions that keep overhead low, profitability is enhanced. By tracking each of these ratios quarter after quarter and year after year, the impact of decisions and strategies are illuminated in these factors.

The second major component of the DuPont formula, **SALES/ASSETS**, is a representation of how frequently the capital of the company is turned over by selling product. Often called capital efficiency or capital turns, this really is a measure of how productive the company is in the use of its capital. If a company can turn its capital over quickly in the generation of sales, it tends to have a better return on its capital.

The classic example of this idea is a grocery store. Grocery stores have very small margins on the products they sell. However, they tend to turn their inventory very quickly (just like the waitress getting multiple turns on her tables per evening). The net result is a better return on assets.

This turnover component is a difficult one to conceptualize, because the link between sales and assets involves the true crossover between the income statement (where sales is the top line) and the balance sheet (where assets measure the totality of what you own).

For years I had a difficult time as a manager trying to figure out how to get my hands around this turnover idea. Ultimately, the small exercise in algebra provided the breakthrough.

**SALES/ASSETS** can also be broken into two components:

$$\frac{\textbf{SALES}}{\textbf{ASSETS}} = \frac{\textbf{SALES}}{\textbf{COGS}} \times \frac{\textbf{COGS}}{\textbf{ASSETS}}$$

In this formulation, the first piece, **SALES/COGS**, is the old retail concept of markup, which is just another way to portray value. In retail, one often takes the cost of a product and applies a markup to the cost to get the sales price. A 50 percent markup would indicate that the cost of the good is multiplied by 1.5 to get the selling price.

Fundamentally, this is just the inverse statement of the value proposition from before (gross margin), which looked at the ratio of what was left over from the selling price (gross), after the cost of goods had been deducted. Both measures look at the value a customer is willing to pay for in a product, compared to the cost of that product. So the management metrics for improvement that applied before (better design, the 7 P's, better buying, etc.) are reflected in this component already. Creating better value and the strategies for improvement that were considered before, carry over to here, also.

The second piece, **COGS/ASSETS**, however, introduces the concept of speed and balance sheet management into our world. The cost of goods sold, as we noted previously, reflects the direct labor and materials needed to create the product being sold. These costs, during the creation of the product, are reflected on the balance sheet as an asset (work in process) until the product is sold and then they are converted back to cash again, to be used to create new product.

The other items on the balance sheet, besides work in process, that make up the assets of the company include cash, accounts receivable, and physical assets such as real estate and machinery, along with office equipment and supplies.

Since the assets of a company are also equal to the total capital of the company, the total assets also reflect the summation of the accounts payable for the company, plus the various forms of debt the company has, plus its equity: both the contributed capital to the company plus any earnings that were retained and "plowed back" into the company.

In simplistic terms, items other than the costs of labor and materials on the balance sheet act as a drag on turnover of capital. If they did not exist and it took a year to create the product, the assets of the company would be equal to the cost of goods sold and the turnover ratio **(COGS/ASSETS)** would be 1.0.

If it took only six months to make the product, the company's money would be used in the first six months to create the product for a sale, the sale would occur, and the capital would be used a second time to make another round of product, which would be sold again. The turnover ratio would be 2.0.

To the extent that there are assets on the balance sheet that do not turn quickly (real estate, machinery, etc.), it takes more "turns of the production wheel" to get an equivalent turnover ratio, because of the friction caused by these slow moving assets.

Now, as a manager, I can begin to understand what to manage. Speed of production is important, first of all. If one can create the products many times in the same year off the same capital base, the turnover ratio gets better. Similarly, really watching what is added to the balance sheet to create "dead" and slow turning assets becomes important. The more dead assets that are added, the harder it is to get high asset turnover and to get a high return on assets. This is the management equivalent of watching what you eat.

If the addition of an asset cannot support an improved capital turn, it must be looked at askance. It is the reason why many companies lease office space, rather than own it or lease machinery rather than own. In each case, the cost of the lease should be less than the drag the dead capital would have on the asset turns of the company. The lease cost, in some cases, becomes part of the cost of goods, driving down the gross margin, and in other cases becomes part of the overhead of the company, driving down the part of gross profit that becomes EBIDTA. In both cases, they impact profitability negatively. The true right answer is whether, in the combination of profitability and asset turns, the return on assets is better one way versus the other.

So, to summarize this second piece of the DuPont formula (**SALES/ASSETS**), we can think of it in two pieces, also. The first is how much value is created when our product is make (expressed by the "markup" of **SALES/COGS**) times how many times in a year we can move COGS through our capital base (**COGS/ASSETS**), with the key driver being our cycle time for making the product and then moving it off the books by selling it and reusing the capital tied up in the inventory again. To the extent that we have to carry a lot of inventory on hand or a lot of raw materials, that inventory is "dead" and hurts our turns.

This truth is why the highly efficient companies of today, such as Toyota and Walmart, focus on lean inventory and just-in-time supply strategies (keeps the dead inventory down) and production cycle time improvement (moves the turns up).

The DuPont formula or model does not necessarily apply to every business, but pieces of it apply to almost all. The formula can be summarized in the following shorthand:

*"You can improve the return on assets of a project or a company by working on reducing overhead, improving margin, and decreasing cycle time. Doing them all together has a dramatic effect. Working on cycle time is the hardest, most in your control, and potentially most rewarding."*

# Acknowledgements

I wish to acknowledge those who have helped me learn the lessons along the way during a career. The understanding of basic writing came from Laura Leonard, my eighth-grade English teacher, and Bob MacDonald, my senior year Advanced Placement English teacher at Cohasset High School, in Cohasset, Massachusetts. My mother, Dorothea Casey, instilled the discipline to keep doing it until you get it right, particularly in schoolwork. My dad, George Casey, every day taught the example of hard work and not giving up.

My professors at Wharton taught the importance of learning after you left school and as you progressed through your career, and the importance of giving back learning to others.

Bob Toll at Toll Brothers provided a culture of the humility needed to know what you did not know and then asking questions until you did. He also showed that humor could be a powerful way to remember lessons.

Tom Maloney, my first superintendent at Toll Brothers, provided the simple wisdom of a genius carpenter and observer of human nature that enabled some of the earliest lessons.

Joe Duckworth and Bob Dwyer at Realen Homes provided some of the great, simple, early examples of how to take wisdom and distill it down into simple and memorable phrases that I began to call my pocket MBA.

Alan Zaring, of Zaring Homes, helped guide me into the world of Total Quality Management, which provided the basis of many of the lessons and observations in the book.

Jim Motta and Dick Larsen at Arvida/St. Joe Company in Florida allowed me to fully experiment with the lessons I had learned in the building of the new city of Weston, Florida. That application of the lessons learned to date allowed more lessons to be learned and then taught to others. Roy Rogers, who handled my government affairs, was a consistent source of knowledge on the drivers that made a master planned community a special place to live.

Keith Christopherson of Christopherson Homes in California provided later life wisdom lessons in the manner of Tom Maloney, two decades earlier.

At DMB in Scottsdale, Aaron Macneil, in copying down the "Georgeisms" over a two-year period, provided the impetus to write the book. Mike DeBell, Charley Freericks, and Wally Graham at DMB provided additional encouragement. Both Aaron and Wally read early drafts of the book and provided valuable commentary and advice.

My friend Lee Smith, retired from *Fortune* and an author in his own right, provided important feedback on form and focus in the early drafts of the book.

Rodney Hall, an executive recruiter at the Talon Group in Dallas, helped me to figure out how to meld this book project with articles I was writing for *Builder Magazine* and how to use new media outlets, including Facebook, LinkedIn, and Twitter, to promote my thinking and writing.

Martin Freedland, my longtime friend and Principal at the Berke Group in Atlanta, has given constant support and encouragement in my acquisition of knowledge and provided a venue to help teach and share that knowledge at his annual Presidential Seminar.

Finally, those who have worked for and with me over several decades deserve mention and attribution. They learned and applied the lessons, helped them to evolve, and have carried the habit of learning and teaching on. In no particular order, and with advance apologies to any left off the list: Rich Rodriguez, Kelly Daniel, Bill Frey, Steve Wackes, Tom Siegel, Chris Drury, Shirley Santiago, Jonathan Rhodes, Jennifer Mahoney, Bob Baker, Rick Hartman, Rich McCormick, Tom Argyris, Kevin Duermit, Jim Boyd, Noelle Tarabulski, Brian Mann, Dan Jones, Pete Hils, Rick Bell, John Hodsdon, Gary Rae, Mike Sutherland, Paul Donaldson, Donny Churchman, Diana Sanger, Lynn Ashton, Jr., Tracy Simmons, Tom Lucas, Derek Earle, Kristi Paganinni, Tom and Caroline Hoyt at McStain, Michael Dickens and Mark Tilley at IBACOS/BuildIQ, and, lastly, to Nick Martell and Hal Davis of Realen.

Thank you.

# About the Author

**George E Casey, Jr.** has worked as an executive in the homebuilding and master planned community development industries for over four decades. Additionally, he has served as a consultant to companies and investors in these industries and as a member of various boards of directors and advisors for companies involved with residential real estate. He is an active member of the Urban Land Institute and an author of articles on subjects involving strategy in residential real estate creation. He is a frequent speaker at industry conferences and seminars on topics involving strategic repositioning of companies and real estate assets as well as improving financial returns of companies through better operational system design. He is a graduate of Rensselaer Polytechnic Institute (Troy, NY) and holds a Masters in Business Administration from the Wharton School of the University of Pennsylvania (Philadelphia, PA).

Readers are encouraged to share their own business lessons learned, stories, and insights on ways people and organizations learn at the website for this book: **www.juicesqueezebook.com**.